THE BROTHERTON COLLECTION

Lord Brotherton
Bronze bust by Ivan Meštrović

THE BROTHERTON COLLECTION

UNIVERSITY OF LEEDS

Its contents described
with illustrations of fifty
books and manuscripts

UNIVERSITY LIBRARY, LEEDS
1986

ISBN 0 902454 07 2

Printed in Great Britain by
W. S. Maney & Son Ltd
Hudson Road, Leeds

Introduction

This publication celebrates the fiftieth anniversary of the arrival in the University of Leeds of its most distinguished separate assembly of rare books and manuscripts, the Brotherton Collection. It is only concerned with that Collection and does not contain information about the books and manuscripts to be found elsewhere in the University Libraries. Detailed information about some of these is available in the series of handlists of manuscripts distributed over many years to selected libraries and in separately published catalogues such as those of the Harold Whitaker Collection of County Atlases (1947), of German literature in the seventeenth and eighteenth centuries (1973 with Supplement 1976), of the Icelandic Collection (1978), and of the Leeds Friends' Old Library and the Birkbeck Library of books dealing with Quakerism (1978 and 1981). A booklet, describing briefly an exhibition of printed books and manuscripts which had been given to the University Library in the hundred years since the University had its beginning, was published in 1974 with the title *A Century of Benefactors*.

The Brotherton Collection is distinguished from the other research collections in the University Library by its separate accommodation, endowment, and purchasing policy. It was in June 1930, when laying the foundation stone of the library building which bears his name and for the construction of which he had provided the money, that Lord Brotherton publicly announced his intention to arrange for his private library to come to the University. That library, together with additions made since his death, forms the Brotherton Collection.

Lord Brotherton, born on 1 April 1856, had from small beginnings built up the largest private chemical manufacturing firm in this country and had become an influential figure in the world of commerce. However, his industrial interests had not absorbed all his energies; he was Member of Parliament for Wakefield in 1902–10 and again in 1918–22; Mayor of Wakefield in 1902–03, Lord Mayor of Leeds in 1913–14 and a Freeman of both cities; Deputy Lieutenant of the West Riding and a Justice of the Peace; Honorary Colonel of the 15th Battalion, the West Yorkshire Regiment, which he raised and equipped at his own expense at the beginning of the 1914–18 war; and a munificent donor to many charities and public institutions. Created a baronet in 1918, he was raised to the peerage as Baron Brotherton of Wakefield in 1929. He died at the age of seventy-four on 21 October 1930, when the Barony became extinct.

As a young man Brotherton had some university experience through attendance at chemistry classes at Owens College, now the University of Manchester. His book collecting did not begin in earnest until 1922. The only fine books which Lord Brotherton is known to have bought before 1922 were two lots at a Christie's Red Cross Sale in April 1917; these comprised first editions of works by George Borrow (now in the Collection) and it is significant that they were undoubtedly bought to indulge the interest in Gypsies of his niece-in-law Dorothy Una Ratcliffe, for it seems that it was the great passion for books of this member of his family which was the original motive force behind Lord Brotherton's collecting.

Dorothy Una Ratcliffe, herself a writer and the friend of writers, had married Brotherton's nephew and business associate Charles Ratcliffe in 1909. Brotherton's own wife had died in 1883 after giving birth to his child who survived only briefly, and Mrs Ratcliffe supported her uncle in many of his public duties. In her statement to the University Council in 1933 about Lord Brotherton's private library (made as Mrs McGrigor Phillips following the breakdown of her first marriage) she recalled how the interest of her uncle-in-law had been drawn to bidding at auction in February 1922 for the Towneley manuscript of the Wakefield cycle of mystery plays. Brotherton's bid was unsuccessful, but after the sale Mrs McGrigor Phillips went with him to Quaritch's bookshop, the bookselling firm which had acted at the auction on his behalf. There they purchased a first edition (1681) of Marvell's poems. Thus Brotherton failed to obtain an important manuscript associated with the city where he had started his chemical company, but acquired an attractive edition of a poet of his adopted county. More important, Lord Brotherton's interest in rare books and manuscripts had been quickened, and in the following months and years he bought on a substantial scale. He soon recognized the necessity of appointing a librarian because, in the words of Mrs McGrigor Phillips, 'expert knowledge of commercial values [was] necessary to build up a great library, as well as a love of fine literature'.

As Lord Brotherton's library expanded, he clearly began to see its broader significance and value for others. By 1926 he seems to have formed the intention to create an independent library for public scholarly use on the model of the John Rylands Library in Manchester and at this time he looked for suitable accommodation for it in the centre of Leeds. This purpose came to no positive result, and the growing collection continued to be housed in extended accommodation at Brotherton's home, Roundhay Hall. In the summer of 1927 Brotherton gave £100,000 to pay for a new library building for the University, and it seems reasonable to suppose that it was at this time that he began to think of the University as a possible future home for his private library. In the event the library came to the University in 1936 to occupy a separate suite of rooms on the first floor of the finished new building, having been presented in accordance with his wish by Brotherton's two residuary legatees, his nephew Charles Ratcliffe Brotherton and Mrs McGrigor Phillips. When transferred the library contained approximately 35,000 printed books and pamphlets, 400 manuscripts, 4,000 deeds, and 30,000 letters. Brotherton was astute enough to realize that his library needed continual development if it was to fulfil the ambitions he had for it. It was his wish that access to it should be accorded to all properly accredited persons and that his collection should 'be held by the University in perpetual trust for the Nation'. Brotherton had bequeathed a sum of £100,000 to the University, and Mrs McGrigor Phillips provided an equivalent endowment by gifts in 1948 and 1956 and a bequest of £25,000 on her death in 1967.

For a variety of reasons little was added to the Collection during the period between Brotherton's death and the end of the Second World War. Since then the Collection has grown significantly, the numbers of printed items and of letters in the original library now having increased by about a half and the number of manuscripts having risen by a factor of ten. Not only have purchases been made with the endowment income but there have been numerous additional gifts from members of the Brotherton family and many others.

This publication seeks to make known the contents of the Collection in 1986 by providing illustrated descriptions of some fifty individual items, selected both for their intrinsic interest and to represent the Collection's main sections, themselves generally described in such detail as is possible here. It is hoped that the volume will thus further promote the use of the Brotherton Collection, an objective so dear to its Founder's heart.

For permission to reproduce copyright material in illustrations, we are grateful to Miss Jennifer Gosse (32); the Estate of Lord Haldane (33); J. C. Hall and the Estate of Keith Douglas (37); and the Estate of John Cowper Powys (38). Thanks are also due to the Photography Section of the University of Leeds Audio-Visual Service for photographing the items illustrated.

The Keeper of the Brotherton Collection has great pleasure in recording his thanks to the following individuals who have generously contributed descriptions of, or information about, books and manuscripts illustrated. The item with which each contributor has particularly been concerned is indicated by the number, in parentheses, that is assigned to it in this volume.

Hugh Aplin, *Leeds Russian Archive, University of Leeds* (46)
Professor W. G. Arnott, *School of Classics, University of Leeds* (48)
Professor John Barnard, *School of English, University of Leeds* (13)
Dr Peter Beal, *Department of Books & Manuscripts, Sotheby's* (21)
Emeritus Professor Francis Berry, *Royal Holloway College, University of London* (38)
Hugh Brogan, *Department of History, University of Essex* (36)
T. A. J. Burnett, *Department of Manuscripts, British Library* (29)
Dr Geoffrey Cantor, *Department of Philosophy, University of Leeds* (23)
Emeritus Professor A. C. Cawley, *School of English, University of Leeds* (9)
Professor David Dilks, *School of History, University of Leeds* (33)
Dr David Fairer, *School of English, University of Leeds* (15)
Dr Frank Felsenstein, *School of English, University of Leeds* (49)
Gordon Forster, *School of History, University of Leeds; President of the Thoresby Society, 1980–85* (42)
Sir Angus Fraser, *Chairman of the Board of Customs and Excise; bibliographer of George Borrow* (45)
Dr Desmond Graham, *School of English, University of Newcastle upon Tyne* (37)
Dr Paul Hammond, *School of English, University of Leeds* (8)

Professor Park Honan, *School of English, University of Leeds* (28)

Professor John Horden, *Centre for Bibliographical Studies, University of Stirling* (10)

Professor G. R. J. Jones, *School of Geography, University of Leeds* (41)

Maurice Kirk, *Department of Social Policy and Health Services Studies, University of Leeds* (22)

Raymond Lister, *President of the Royal Society of Miniature Painters, Sculptors and Gravers, 1970–80* (34)

Emeritus Professor Ronald Martin, *School of Classics, University of Leeds* (5)

David I. Masson, *formerly Sub-Librarian, Brotherton Collection, University of Leeds* (12)

Professor Jane Millgate, *Department of English, University of Toronto* (25)

Professor Michael Millgate, *Department of English, University of Toronto* (35)

Leslie A. Morris, *Rosenbach Museum & Library, Philadelphia* (20)

Russell Mortimer, *formerly Senior Sub-Librarian, Brotherton Library, University of Leeds* (19)

Tom Paulin, *Department of English Studies, University of Nottingham* (40)

Dr O. S. Pickering, *Brotherton Library, University of Leeds* (3)

Dr John Pitcher, *St John's College, University of Oxford* (7)

Alan Ross, *Editor of the* London Magazine (39)

Professor Julian Rushton, *Department of Music, University of Leeds* (47)

Joseph W. Scott, *Emeritus Librarian, University College London* (1)

John Taylor, *School of History, University of Leeds* (2)

Ann Thwaite, *biographer of Sir Edmund Gosse* (32)

Dr Christopher Todd, *Department of French, University of Leeds* (17)

Emeritus Professor William Walsh, *School of English, University of Leeds* (26)

The publication owes most to Christopher Sheppard, Sub-Librarian in the University Library, Leeds.

D. Cox
University Librarian and
Keeper of the Brotherton Collection

Contents

The items illustrated are arranged in groups representing major sections of the Brotherton Collection and are selected to show the variety of material within those sections.

EIGHTEENTH-CENTURY ENGLISH LITERATURE

OTHER SEVENTEETH- AND EIGHTEENTH-CENTURY WRITING

NINETEENTH-CENTURY ENGLISH LITERARY MANUSCRIPTS

THE NOVELLO-COWDEN CLARKE COLLECTION

THE BROTHERTON COLLECTION

1. A HISTORY OF THE WORLD

Illuminated manuscript roll on vellum, France, late fifteenth century.

This manuscript is written in Anglo-Norman French on a vellum roll of 39 membranes measuring 17.6 metres long. It is written in *lettres batârdes* in four columns (mostly), illustrated with 64 circular medallions, varying between 56mm and 75mm in diameter. The prologue begins 'Cy sensuit la genealogie de la bible': the first double column begins 'In principio creauit deus celum et terram'.

Across the head of the roll stretch contingent miniatures, each 70mm in diameter giving six unusual days of the Creation: Comment dieu crea le ciel la terre & les estoilles; Comment dieu crea la terre les herbes et les abres . . .; Comment dieu crea les eaues et les poissons . . .; Comment dieu crea les bestes et les oiseaulx . . .; Comment dieu crea les anges . . .; Comment dieu trebucha les maulvais anges . . .. Then follow the remaining 58 medallions showing: creation of Adam and Eve, Eve tempted by the serpent, Adam and Eve break God's commandment, Adam and Eve expelled, Adam delves, Noah's Ark, Tower of Babylon, Abraham, Joshua, the fall of Troy, departure of the Trojan ships (Aeneas, Priamus, Turtus, Helenus), David. Here the roll expands to four columns — religious history, Roman history, French history, English history: Brut kills the giants, destruction of Samaria, foundation of Sincambria, Zedekiah, slaughter of Nebuchadnezzar, Romulus building Rome, building of Paris [Lutesse], fall of Babylon, killing of Baltasar, rape of the Sabine women, Queen Vashti, Alexander the Great, Judas Machabeus, the Nativity, the Ascension, New Troy named London, Jesus Christ became man as first Pope, murder of Julius Caesar, the Sincambrians named Gaul France, the French discovered the Roumanians, the first ordination of archbishops and bishops, Conan, King of Brittany, Pharamond, King of France, baptism of King Clovis, the English king killed 30 Bretons, Dagobert founded the church of S. Denis, death of King Arthur, Great Britain destroyed by the Africans, given to the Saxons, and named England, Pepin, King of France, S. Gregory, Pope, William the Bastard conquered England [this miniature has been roughly torn out], Hugh Capet, King of France, Godfrey de Bouillon voyages to conquer the Holy Land, Charlemagne, Emperor of Rome and France, Godfrey de Bouillon, King of Jerusalem, S. Louis, Beranger, Philip de Valois, King of France, Edward, King of England, Jehan, King of France, captured at Poitiers [1356], Charles V, Charles VI asked for aid from his people. The text now expands across the full breadth of the roll: Charles VII, died 1461, Louis XI.

Twenty-seven medieval manuscripts in the Brotherton Collection, including that illustrated here, are listed with full and scrupulous descriptions in the third volume of the late Dr N. R. Ker's Medieval Manuscripts in British Libraries, *1983, to which the interested reader is warmly referred. All but two of these manuscripts date from the fifteenth and early sixteenth centuries, with examples written in England, France, the Low Countries, Italy, Germany and, evidently, Spain. The two exceptions are both twelfth-century manuscripts, Cicero,* De officiis, *written in Italy, and Bede* In epistolas canonicas, *written in southern Germany.*

Comment le roy artus conquist
plusieurs pais et comment il occist m
morded le traistre et comment il
mourut. &c

44

Apres uterpendragon
fut fait roy son filz le
noble roy artus qui puis
sement regna il estoit
ieune de .xv. ans et avoit en luy tou
te bonte et vainquit ses ennemis et
conquist hyrlande escoce france et

2. THE ANONIMALLE CHRONICLE

Manuscript on vellum, England, late fourteenth century.

The *Anonimalle chronicle*, which extends from the time of the legendary Brutus to 1381, has claims to be considered the most important chronicle written in northern England during the later Middle Ages. Composed in French towards the end of the fourteenth century by an anonymous monk of St Mary's, York, the chronicle draws for the latter part of its narrative upon a variety of sources. These include the most detailed description of a medieval parliament known to survive (that of the Good Parliament of 1376), and an unusually well informed account of the Peasants' Revolt (1381). Both passages were undoubtedly the work of an eye-witness. Although they are unlikely to be the original composition of a York monk, the manner in which these accounts found their way into a northern chronicle has never been satisfactorily explained.

In the main section from Brutus to 1307 the chronicle has been described as a variant version of the popular history known as the French prose *Brut*. Its narrative none the less differs considerably from that of the prose *Brut*. It utilises a number of monastic accounts, and reveals an interest in early ecclesiastical history which is not found in the *Brut*. From 1307 to 1333 the *Anonimalle chronicle* falls into the main *Brut* tradition, and contains the fullest text of the shorter of the two standard continuations with which the prose *Brut* was furnished. The continuation has a pronounced London interest, going into detail on the Londoners' reaction to the crisis of 1326. The text contains a number of Franciscan and York interpolations. After 1333 the *Anonimalle chronicle* is an individual account, drawing upon a variety of missing sources, possibly of London origin.

The history of the manuscript itself is of some interest. In the sixteenth century the chronicle was known to antiquaries in London such as Thynne and Stow (a note by whom, 'Liber S. Mary in York as may be supposed' appears in the margin of the folio reproduced). Thynne gave the chronicle the original version of its name ('an anonimalle chronicle'). The manuscript appears to have moved between Yorkshire and London in the late sixteenth and early seventeenth centuries, and it was almost certainly at this time that it came into the possession of the Ingilby family at Ripley, where it was rediscovered among their records only in 1920. In 1927 the section of the chronicle from 1333 to 1381 was edited by Professor V. H. Galbraith and this part of the text was immediately recognised as constituting an historical narrative of first rate historical value. The manuscript was purchased in the 1920s by Mr H. L. Bradfer-Lawrence and in recent years has been deposited on loan at the Fitzwilliam Museum, Cambridge. It was acquired by the Brotherton Collection in 1982.

The Anonimalle Chronicle is one of two medieval manuscripts we have acquired since Dr Ker surveyed the Collection. The other is an early fifteenth-century prayer book, also probably written in Yorkshire, for use at Beverley Minster. Formerly owned by the Marquis of Bute, it is notable for having the offices duplicated, being recorded once for the Use of Sarum and again for the Use of York.

egrement les enchasist od ses gentz bien a .iiij. leukes. De
Calais a grant plente de ses enemys prist e occist. Et adonges
le dit Capitayn de Calais e ovesqe lui touz les puissantz de
la dite ville pur doute qils avoient del Roi dengleterre e aussi pur

[margin: ... de Calise]

la graunde famyne qils avoient deschauces e deschemises od cordes
entour lour coles vindrent al dit Roi dengleterre e donerent al dit
ensegne (?) e lui rendrent la dite ville. Et le dit capitayn lui bailla
touz les cleves de les portes del ville e se mistrent en sa grace
e prierent de lour vies salver. Et le Roi qe tut fort avoit este
grevous e irrable les graunta vie e membre e les comaunda
al tour de Londres. Adonges le Roi entra la ville de Calais od
ses seignours ovesqe lui e illoeques demura trois iours auxint (?)
qe les ... purroient entrer e puis delivera a sire Johan de
Chaunceston la ville de Calais a garder e governer e le
chastell a sire Thomas de Kingeston e puis repaira en
Engleterre ovesqe touz les seignours dengleterre queux furent ovesqe
lui en sa guerre. Amaintenant nostre seignour tut puissant demonstra
de sa graunde congnesse (?). Lan de grace M.CCC.xlviij. entour le

[margin: La grant mortalite ...]

fest de seint Piere ad vincula comencea la grant mortalite en
Engleterre a Bristowe par marchauntz e mariners e endura en la
south partie dans les parties de Bristowe tout le August
e tut le ... Et en lan apres cest assavoir M.CCC.xlix. la dite
pestilence comencea en les autres parties dengleterre e endura
tut lan entier issint qe a peine les vives ne purroient ensevelir

[margin: [illegible]]

les mortz. Lan de grace M.CCC.xlix. lendemayn apres le fest
de seint Barnabe apostle mons. sire Leonel de Andewerpe
mons. sire Johan de Gaunt e mons. sire Edmund de Langley
les fitz a tres noble Roi dengleterre Edward le tierce furent
receux en la fraternite e les prieres de les moignes del
Abbeie nostre Dame de Everwik souz lour chapitre dan Thomas
de Multon adonges Abbe e present de mesme le lieu a lour
propre volunte e requeste. Mesme cel an entour le fest del
Purificacioun de nostre Dame un Chivaler de Fraunce qi
Emery de Pavy nome demurant od le Roi dengleterre en la
chapitenship de Calais faussement e par tresoun vendist
le chastel de Calais a les Fraunceis pur grant somme dor.
Et le dit sire Emery garnist le Roi dengleterre e les Engleis a
lour avantage. Et le Roi assigne les traitours qe furent par les Fraunceis

[illegible]

3. AN ANTHOLOGY OF RELIGIOUS VERSE AND PROSE

Manuscript on paper, England, early fifteenth century.

This anthology of Middle English religious verse and prose was put together in the first half of the fifteenth century by a single scribe writing at different times. Its interest arises partly from its mix of contents, partly from the seemingly personal manner in which some of the items are introduced, and partly from the problem of determining the original number and arrangement of items: many leaves are now missing, and others are bound in the wrong order.

The manuscript begins with the long and very popular didactic poem *The Pricke of Conscience*. Thereafter the contents are mainly prose works of a devotional or instructional nature, many (like Richard Lavynham's *A Litil Tretys on the Seven Deadly Sins* or the extracts from the English verson of the *Stimulus amoris*) well-known from other manuscripts, others (including a Miracle of the Virgin and a Form of Confession) of apparently more restricted circulation. There is some narrative material, notably a sequence of the Passion and Resurrection of Christ, and (in verse) two legends of the Holy Cross.

Much of the book seems intended to be a manual of moral or doctrinal teaching. Parts of it read as if specially composed for a particular person, not yet grown up. 'O þou my brothyr þat art yong of age qwiche kanst not confesse thiself onto thy gostly fadyr' writes the scribe on f.82r, proceeding to give detailed instructions about confession, with the same pupil continually in mind. In the same vein the preamble to *The Gast of Gy* (f.92r) claims the work was specially translated into English 'for þe more intelleccion for the [my frend] þat canst no latyn'. Later, among other examples, we find 'O þou my frend y wyll teche þea lityll lesson how þou shal loue god' (f.115v, reproduced opposite).

Other items, however, begin impersonally or abruptly, and for several reasons it is likely that the scribe was copying the personal-sounding material unchanged from an exemplar rather than himself composing and translating for a 'frend' or 'brothyr'. Nevertheless he has left us a fascinating book, written in a practised hand of some distinction (enhanced by different kinds of script, decorated initials, and the frequent use of red ink) in a dialect that has been localised in south Lincolnshire. Who he was is unknown. He may be the M.R. of the 'secundum M.R.' on f.67v, or this, too, may have been conscientiously copied from an exemplar.

The Collection has two other medieval manuscripts in English, one consisting almost entirely of a second text of The Pricke of Conscience *(of which in all some 115 medieval manuscripts survive, nearly double the number for Chaucer's* Canterbury Tales*). This manuscript, perhaps earlier than that illustrated, written on vellum and in a Worcestershire dialect, assigns authorship of the poem to Robert Grosseteste, Bishop of Lincoln; this is evidently an anachronism, for he died in 1253, well before one of the poem's sources appeared. Our third English manuscript, of about 1450, is undoubtedly by John Mirk — his* Festial*, a collection of homilies written before 1415 for the clergy. This again was a popular work of which numerous other manuscripts are extant.*

O þu my frend y wyll teche þe a lytyll lesson how þu shal loue god & for sterr
thy self to kyndele thin herte i to his loue. Which lesson ys callyd Stimulus amoris. drawyn of Bonauenture cardynal & doctor.

Zyf þu wylt ben steryd for to loue god. knowe this ferst. þat ther
ys nothing þt more kyndelyth a mans herte. than devout thin-
kyng of the grete zyftis of god. fforqwy thorwz largesse of his
zyftis frely zouyn to the is opinly shewyd a ful tokyn that he lovyth the
And what is more steryng to the for to loue him. þan for to vndyrstond
and fele sothfastly þt he lovyth the. Sothly nothing more. fforqwy vy-
cious men þt arn most felle zit they lovyn kyndely them. þt lovyn them.
Therfor sethe it ys so. þt god lovyth the frely and shewyth the kyndnesse
and goodnes loue him azen. ¶ Go to him wt trust of herte. and think
þt þu art hys. and not thin owne. prees vppon him & offre thiself to him as
his creatur. þt for his owne loue he made & bowght the thorw his bytt-
passyon. And thynke þt þu stondist evyr byfore him i his sight. as yf þu were
i heuyn. And make nomore dowte. þt whatsomeuer þu askyst of him me-
kely þt longith to thy soule hele he wyl gyue yt. fforqwy he is leef for
to helpe þe. þt is al his desyre azens the. ffor wh. qwan þu forzat him &
thorwz senne wylfully despysid him. zit he suffrid þe. And þu smette him
and wowndyd him i manyr as a wood sik man smytith a leche that wolde hele him. zyt he forbare the. and azens thi wylle steryd the for to wylle
to leue synne & serue him. ¶ As for what perylys for what myschef-
nys & for what sennys hath he delyueryd the. I hope þu can not rekne
alle. whi dede he þus to the. sothly for none othyr cause. but for he lo-
vid the. why wylt þu not therfor loue him azen. Thow wylt loue a man
greetly. yyf he zeue the a lytil worldly good or zef he do the a kynde tur-
n. How is it thanne þt þu lovyst him not meche more þt wyll forzeue þe
all thy trespas. & wyll zeue the himself to thy mede. zyf þu loue thy
owne self. why lovyst not hym þt made thyself. Thou hast dystroyd
thiself thorwz senne. and every day dystroyest. & zit þu lovyst thiself.
and lovyst not þan him þt hath made the and restoryd the and kepith þe.
what dost þu man. whi lovyst þu him not. Ryse vp and stere thin herte for
to loue him and sey to him þus. O lord y am thi creatur and the only
y coueyte. & þfor þu may not deyne thiself to me. thus shalt þu thanke sadly
& vnbydyngly. and rekne vp as moche wrechidnes and onkyndenes
as þu can of thyself and as moche goodnes & kyndenes as þu can of hym.
And zif þu do thus it is wondyr but thi herte be steryd and kyndelyd
to loue him. What man zif he thoghte this inwardly myght wtholde
him. þt he ne wolde forzete alle othyr thingis. and fully kast him for to
plese god. Whan he thinkith hou hym thi lord þt is angelys delycis & mede
of blyssid soulys. proferth himself to a wrecchid man ful of synne and
of corrupcon. fforqwy be a man nevyr so foule a synnere. ze powz
he stynke i custom of senne as lazar stank i his grave. zitt zif he turne
him to god & aske mercy. he shal haue yt. ffor he seith himself þus aske.
and ye shal haue. Wherto turnyn we oure hertis. and ovyr trauaylyn
our bodyes abowtyn worldly thyng. whan we may haue the maker
of alle. What seke we more. sithe we may haue so lyghtly yf we wol
þe souereyn lord cryst ihc. Wherto ar we so besy aboute sekyng of nyght
noght

No [margin, beside "i heuyn. And make nomore dowte"]

No bn [margin, beside "of corrupcon fforqwy be a man"]

4. EUCLID (*fl. c.* 300 B.C.)

Elementa, *Venice, 1482.*

This was the first substantial mathematical book to be printed with geometrical figures. The printer was Erhard Ratdolt, a native of Augsburg who worked for ten years in Venice, where the Euclid was printed; he refers in the preface with pride to his success in printing diagrams and thus overcoming the difficulties which had previously dissuaded printers from issuing important books the intelligibility of which depended on such diagrams. Practically nothing is known about the life of Euclid, although it is clear that he taught and wrote in Alexandria about 300 B.C.. The Latin version printed here is by the Italian Johannes Campanus, dates from the thirteenth century, and derives in part from an Arabic text. The translation of Euclid from the Arabic owes much to an Englishman, Adelard of Bath, who was active at the beginning of the twelfth century. The Greek text was not printed till 1533.

Lord Brotherton acquired about 250 books printed before 1500, a very small proportion of the astonishingly large number published during the first half-century of printing, but enough to provide examples of many subject categories and of many famous presses. Valuable, also, to the student of early printing are the sets of single leaves from many books assembled by Konrad Haebler or Wilhelm Schreiber. Of the first substantial book to be printed with moveable types, the so-called Gutenberg Bible, there is only one leaf, but there are four complete fifteenth-century Bibles including the 1478 (Nuremberg) edition of Koberger and the Basle edition of 1498 with the commentary of Nicholas de Lyra. Writings of the Christian Fathers form a large group, and the editions of St Augustine's De Civitate Dei *include those of Spira (1470) and Jenson (1475). Classical authors include Aristotle, Cicero, Horace, Livy, Lucan, Ovid, Pliny, Plutarch (an especially fine copy of the* editio princeps *of the Lives), Seneca, and Terence.*

Illustrated books include Breydenbach's Journey to the Holy Land (Mainz, 1486) with folding plates of views of towns; the Schatzbehalter (1491) with fine woodcuts of biblical subjects, besides the world history commonly called the Nuremberg Chronicle (1492) — both these printed by Koberger; and Brant's Ship of Fools (Basle, 1497) in the Latin adaptation by Jacob Locher but including most of the original woodcuts. Other incunabula of particular interest are two editions of the popular encyclopedia On the Properties of Things by the thirteenth-century Franciscan, Bartholomaeus Anglicus (Lyons, 1480 in Latin and Toulouse, 1494 in Spanish); the treatise on music by Boethius (Venice, 1492) which has been described as the first work of musical theory in the Christian West and, incidentally, is liberally illustrated with diagrams; and the Practica musicae *(Brescia, 1497) of Gaffurius (1451–1522), the eminent Italian theoretician of music and composer.*

Finally may be mentioned three books on astronomy and astrology, all of which were widely known and read. Two, like the Euclid here illustrated, were printed by Ratdolt, namely the Poetica astronomica *attributed to the Roman, Hyginus (Venice, 1482) and the* Flores astrologiae *of the Arab, Albumasar (Augsburg, 1488). The third, the treatise on the sphere of John of Holywood (Sacrobosco), was almost certainly more attractive to Lord Brotherton because its author may have been born in Halifax, and Brotherton's loyalty to his adopted county was very strong.*

Preclarissimus liber elementorum Euclidis perspi/
cacissimi: in artem Geometrie incipit quãfoelicissime:

Punctus est cuius ps nõ est. ¶ Linea est
lõgitudo sine latitudine cui⁹ quidẽ ex/
tremitates sſt duo pũcta. ¶ Linea recta
ẽ ab vno pũcto ad aliũ breuissima extẽ/
sio i extremitates suas vtrũqʒ eoꝝ reci
piens. ¶ Supficies ẽ q̃ lõgitudinẽ ⁊ lati
tudinẽ tm̃ hȝ: cui⁹ termĩ quidẽ sũt linee.
¶ Supficies plana ẽ ab vna linea ad a/
liã extẽsio i extremitates suas recipiẽs
¶ Angulus planus ẽ duarũ linearũ al/
ternus ꝯtactus: quaꝝ expãsio ẽ sup sup/
ficiẽ applicatioqʒ nõ directa. ¶ Quãdo aũt angulum ꝯtinẽt due
linee recte rectiline⁹ angulus noĩat. ¶ Qñ recta linea sup rectã
steterit duoqʒ anguli vtrobiqʒ fuerit eq̃les: eoꝝ vterqʒ rect⁹ erit
¶ Lineaqʒ linee supstãs ei cui supstat ꝑpendicularis vocat. ¶ An
gulus vo qui recto maior ẽ obtusus dicit. ¶ Angul⁹ vo minor re
cto acut⁹ appellat. ¶ Termin⁹ ẽ qd vniuscuiusqʒ finis ẽ. ¶ Figura
ẽ q̃ tmino vl' termis ꝯtinẽt. ¶ Circul⁹ ẽ figura plana vna q̃dem li/
nea ꝯtẽta: q̃ circũferentia noĩat: in cui⁹ medio pũct⁹ ẽ: a quo oẽs
linee recte ad circũferẽtiã exeũtes sibiĩuicẽ sũt equales. Et hic
quidẽ pũct⁹ cẽtrũ circuli dr̃. ¶ Diameter circuli ẽ linea recta que
sup ei⁹ centꝝ trãsiens extremitatesqʒ suas circũferẽtie applicans
circulũ i duo media diuidit. ¶ Semicirculus ẽ figura plana dia/
metro circuli ⁊ medietate circũferentie ꝯtenta. ¶ Portio circu/
li ẽ figura plana recta linea ⁊ parte circũferẽtie ꝯtẽta: semicircu/
lo quidẽ aut maior aut minor. ¶ Rectilinee figure sũt q̃ rectis li/
neis cõtinent quarũ quedã trilatere q̃ trib⁹ rectis lineis: quedã
quadrilatere q̃ q̃tuor rectis lineis: q̃dã mltilatere que pluribus
q̃ʒ quatuor rectis lineis continent. ¶ Figurarũ trilaterarũ: alia
est triangulus hñs tria latera equalia. Alia triangulus duo hñs
eq̃lia latera. Alia triangulus triũ inequalium laterũ. Haꝝ iterũ
alia est orthogoniũ: vnũ. s. rectum angulum habens. Alia ẽ am/
bligonium aliquem obtusum angulum habens. Alia est oxigoni
um: in qua tres anguli sunt acuti. ¶ Figurarũ autẽ quadrilateraꝝ
Alia est q̃dratum quod est equilaterũ atqʒ rectangulũ. Alia est
tetragon⁹ long⁹: q̃ est figura rectangula: sed equilatera non est.
Alia est helmuaym: que est equilatera: sed rectangula non est.

De principijs p se notis: ⁊ pmo de diffini/
tionibus earundem.

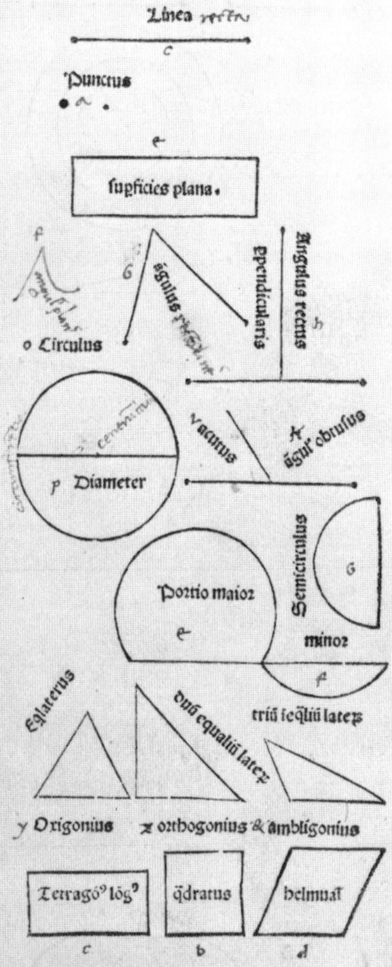

5. LORENZO GUGLIELMO TRAVERSAGNI (1425–1503)

Epitome margaritae eloquentiae, *London, [c. 1480].*

The unique printed copy of Traversagni's *Epitome* was rediscovered in 1952 by Mrs Jean Mortimer of the Brotherton Library in a composite volume of incunabula in the Library of Ripon Cathedral. Since the *Epitome* had suffered considerable damage from damp, it was removed from the volume in which it was contained, and repaired and rebound in vellum by the binding staff of the British Museum. It was bought for the Brotherton Collection at Sotheby's on 21 May 1960.

Typographical evidence establishes that the *Epitome* was printed by William Caxton in his type 2*, probably in 1480 or 1481. The work, which is without title-page, consists of 34 leaves with 29 lines to a full page. There are neither head-lines nor quire signatures, but line endings are even, and it may be one of the first of Caxton's works to show this feature. The colophon on 34 recto states that the *Epitome* was written by Laurentius Gulielmus de Saona in the University of Paris in January 1480. This Franciscan humanist, otherwise Lorenzo Guglielmo Traversagni, was born at Savona in Italy in 1425. Between 1450 and 1487 he travelled and lectured widely in Europe. During the years 1476 to 1482 he spent much of his time in England, and in July 1478, while at Cambridge, he completed the manuscript of his *Margarita eloquentie castigate ad eloquendum diuina accomodata*, commonly known by the title given to it by Caxton in his printed edition of 1479 (?) as the *Nova rhetorica*. It is this work that the *Epitome* professes to epitomize.

The importance of Traversagni's two rhetorical works lies in the way he seeks to adapt the teaching of classical models (chiefly the anonymous treatise *Ad Herennium* and Cicero's *De inuentione*) to the needs of contemporary eloquence; to that end classical precepts are extensively illustrated by passages from the Bible. So, in the page illustrated (f.21v), in a long continuous passage, transcribed almost verbatim from Cicero, *De inuentione* I 104–5, there are inserted examples from Ezechiel 16. 31–3, I Samuel 8. 6, II Samuel 13. 12ff. and Esther 1. 16ff.

The most striking typographical features are the abbreviation of some common Latin words or word-endings; so '-t' with a feathered crossbar for '-tur' (lines 3 and 29), an elongated '9' for '-us' (line 4 and *passim*), and abbreviations of '-que' (line 5 etc.), 'quam' (line 9) and 'quod' (line 18); see also the abbreviations for 'supra' (before 'contra' in line 14) and for '-rum' (at the beginning of line 18).

There were two English incunabula in Lord Brotherton's original collection. The earlier is a compilation by John Wotton of devotional literature entitled Speculum Christiani, *printed in about 1486 by William de Machlinia, who came from Mechelen between Brussels and Antwerp. The other is* The Chastising of God's Children, *printed in about 1492 by Wynkyn de Worde, who took over Caxton's business and materials after his death. It is another devotional work in English and has the added interest of being one of the earliest English books to have a separate title-page. Details of these and our other incunabula, excepting the Caxton* Epitome, *appear in* The Brotherton Library. A Catalogue of Ancient Manuscripts and Early Printed Books, *1931.*

quam dicit. Non facta es quasi meretrix fastidiosa au=
gens precium sed quasi mulier adultera que super virũ
suum inducit alienos Omnibus meretricibus dant mer
cedes. tu autem dedisti mercedes cunctis amatorib9 tuis.
aut donabas eis vt intrarent ad te vndiqz ad forni=
candum tecum. Decimus locus est p quẽ oĩa que in ne
gocio acta sunt que eciam post negociũ cõsequuta cũ vni
uscuiusqz indignatione criminose colligim9 et rem ante
oculos eius apud quem dicitur verbis et signis q̃ maxime
ponim9 vt id quod indignum est illis coram quibus dici
tur perinde videatur indignum ac si ipsi interfuissent ac
vidissent hui- loco deseruiunt colores sentenciarum effe=
ctio Imago tatio seruitiuo et demonstratiuo hoc eciam
loco vsus est -e sech. vbi ẽ contra isrl. Vndecim9 locus
est p quem ostendimus ab e- factum esse p quez minime
oportuerit et a quo si ali9 faceret prohiberi queieret quale
fuit peccatum Inde contra domum scribarum eciã et pha=
riseorum. Duodecim9 locus est p quem indignamur q̃ hoc
nobis primo acciderit neqz alicui ante vsu euenit quo lo=
co vti potuit Samuel propheta petentem sibi regem dari
primi Reg. vj. Decimustercius locus est p quẽ quãdo in
iuria diurantur contumelie coniuncta quo vti potuisset
Thamar contra Amon fratrem qui defloraverat eam. ij
Regũ. xiij. Decimusquartus locus est p quem petimus
ab his qui audiunt vt ad res suas nostras referant iniu
rias si ad pueros pertinebit de liberis suis cogitent. si ad
mulieres de vxoribus. si ad senes de patribus et parenti=
bus hoc communicacit- r fit per primum colorem sentencia
rum qui dicit distributio de hoc loco usus ẽ Mancha dux

6. PATRICK CARY (1623?–1657)

Ballades dedicated to the Lady Victoria Uvedale, *autograph manuscript, 1652/53.*

Until this elegant volume dated 1652/53 became known in 1984, the poems of Patrick Cary were to be found in a single autograph manuscript dated 1651, formerly owned by Sir Walter Scott and still preserved at Abbotsford. Scott published the 37 poems in his manuscript as *Trivial Poems and Triolets* in 1819. Between that date and 1978, when Sister Veronica Delany published her modern edition of Cary's work, much was learnt of the author's life and career — his unsettled expatriate Roman Catholic youth, his return to England and the Anglican Church, his official appointments in Ireland before an early death — but Sister Veronica, too, knew only the one manuscript.

The recently discovered volume adds no major new poem to the Cary canon; indeed, although it is in an early binding, it is clearly incomplete in itself and contains only 13 of Cary's 24 secular poems and none of the religious ones. However, what is strikingly new is that each poem is preceded by an illustration by Cary, with a couplet caption, and is followed by a smaller design; in the Abbotsford manuscript only the religious poems have some emblematic illustration. Further, many of the poems in the later manuscript have minor verbal changes by the author as well as variations throughout in punctuation, spelling and capitalization which the future editor must consider. The order of poems is also altered, placing them in two general thematic groups. The manuscript has a title-page adorned with coats of arms and the final page is meticulously inscribed 'Ballades composed, and transcribed by Iohn-Patricke Carey, when Hee had little else to doe'.

The Collection also has autograph poems by Alexander Pope, James Thomson and Edward Young, and, from an earlier period, Sir Thomas Wroth's 'sad encomion' on his wife Margaret, 1635, a copy for her brother Sir Nathaniel Rich with a detailed prose account of her death. Pope's poem is a short translation from Boethius, c. *1703, for Sir William Trumbull, whose own parallel translation is with it. Thomson's is an early humorous poem 'Lisy's parting with her cat',* c. *1720, while Young's presents his* The Universal Passion, *1728, to the first Duke of Chandos. Marvell, Davenant and Prior are represented by autograph letters, Milton by autograph corrections to another.*

Other examples of autograph poetry from this period include verse notebooks by William Fairfax (1593–1621) and by his later kinsman Henry Fairfax, son of the fourth lord; both belonged to Sir Thomas Phillipps. Symon Jory's long poem 'The perfect mans practice', c. *1630, was written during imprisonment and dedicated to Sir Julius Caesar. Works dated from 1629 to 1654, evidently in one William Thomson's hand, include devotional poems and a prose essay in spiritual autobiography. Likewise, the prose religious musings of Castilian Morris, Town Clerk of Leeds from 1684, are interspersed with his poems, including acrostics and some designed for visual effect. A large volume of verse by Sir Philip Wodehouse M.P. and his son Sir Edmund dates from 1664 to 1715 and of two by the organist Henry Hall the elder, one may be autograph. Over 100 unpublished poems by Thomas Fitzgerald accompany his fair copy of his* Poems on Several Occasions, *1733.*

Though pinching; WANT were not soe Ill a Thing,
Deiectednesse, and Scorne did Itt not bring.

DICKE.

IACKE! nay preethee come away!
This is noe time for sadnesse;
PAN's cheife Feast is kept to day,
Each Shepeard shewes his gladnesse:
W'are to meete All on the Greene,
To dance, and sport together;
O what Brau'ry will bee seene!
I hope t'will proue fayre Weather!

2. Looke! I'ue gott a new

7. SAMUEL DANIEL (1562–1619) *attributed author*

Manuscript copies of four poems and a letter, c. 1620–39.

This twenty-page folio manuscript contains four unsigned verse epistles and a prose letter, all transcribed in a single italic hand dating from the first half of the seventeenth century. The recipients of the poems are Henry, Prince of Wales (d. 1612), a certain 'Sir R.C.', Anne, Lady Harington (d. 1621), and an anonymous lady, to whom the lines illustrated are addressed. The letter, again unsigned, is addressed to a great lord, who has been identified on internal evidence as Robert Carr, Earl of Somerset, King James's favourite, who in 1616 was tried and convicted for the murder of Sir Thomas Overbury. The poems and prose have been dated, again on internal evidence, as written between 1609 and 1616, and it has been argued that they form a group of unpublished pieces by the poet Samuel Daniel. The attribution is now widely accepted; in *English* (Summer 1982), the epistles were described by Martin Dodsworth as 'fine, late examples of Daniel's art'. Daniel is best known for his Elizabethan poetry, but his later writings, especially *Musophilus* and the verse epistles, represent his most notable achievement; in them, as C. S. Lewis observed, he 'actually thinks in verse: thinks deeply, arduously' and so makes himself 'the most interesting man of letters of his century'.

Not many of Daniel's manuscripts have survived, and so it is fortunate that the Brotherton Collection has another, which is also of special interest. In this Daniel has altered his famous verse epistle to Lady Cumberland (which Wordsworth so admired) to suit another lady at the Jacobean court.

The manuscript illustrated was recognised as almost certainly Daniel's work by Dr John Pitcher when he saw it exhibited in the Brotherton Collection as a new acquisition. It is hoped that other anonymous individual items here will have similarly welcome identification. However, the authorship of many, though they are not autograph, is already known or cogently argued; a few examples may be mentioned.

A recently acquired Latin grammar of about 1680 by Lewis Maidwell, educationalist and playwright, is prefaced by two poems, respectively by 'J. Drydon' and Nahum Tate; the former, if by John Dryden, would be the first 'new' Dryden poem found for a century. Dryden's connections with Maidwell, like his links with Tate, are well known and echoes of Dryden's other work appear in the poem; only its indifferent quality, which might indicate a great writer's casual occasional piece, prompts caution in the ascription.

Two long poems by Sir William Davenant, first published in 1673, appear in fuller form in a manuscript dated 1678, apparently copied from drafts Davenant sent to Lord Mordaunt; we also have one of the copies of the 1651 quarto of Gondibert *with Davenant's corrections in manuscript. A manuscript of* Mercurius Mennippeus, *often credited to the author of* Hudibras, *is here signed 'Winniard Johann. Oxon' (presumably Thomas Winnard of St John's College), while the relationship between our eight late seventeenth-century manuscripts of Samuel Colvil's hudibrastic* Mock Poem *remains to be established. From rather later, we have a volume of unpublished poems by Sneyd Davies, 'beatified before his time' according to his young friend Anna Seward, and a revised proof of his poems in John Whaley's* Collection of Original Poems and Translations, *1745.*

Since god hath in his mightie providence
Sett you uppon a Mountaine of your owne . .
From whence you may wth safe magnificence
Into th'ocean of this world looke downe.
And see the wracks that prowd adventurers
make on the rocks, and haue therein no share.
Behold the billow's of Ambitious stirrs ;
That toss them to and fro, with toilsome care .
And what retourne they make, who speede the best
what rents they haue, what weather beaten harts
whilst you may with an vndecoivd brest
Enioy the blessings . wch your peace imparts .
And be spectator of the roles they act .
who personate uppon this stage of Court .
And note wth what poore cuning they compact
All their disguisings, howe their shiftings sort
what risings, what deiections, grace, disgrace
How egar chacers come, pursued in chace .
Then who they are, from whence, for what advanc
That outstart other men in dignitie .
And how the price of weakness is inhanced ,
Aboue desert, and worth, and industrie .
Then wth what pleasant phrensies, merry madnesses
They entertained are, with all, and home .
Appearing not in their owne visages .
They all weare masks, and onlie are in shew .
where Madam by how much the more yu striue
To shew your self, the lesser you appeare .
The throng and press, yor virtue doth depriue
of th'honor you might haue, were you but cleere ;
The place afords not roome to shew your good
wch th'open plaines illustrate not a wood .
Beside's all heare in like opinion stand .
And of one note, markt wth the self same brand .
For howsoever greatnes may be cleere .
Yet here it never is esteemd sincere ,

8. A POETICAL MISCELLANY

Manuscript miscellany of copies of poems by Dryden and others, c. 1680–95.

In the reign of Charles II many poems circulated in manuscript rather than in print; obscene and libellous material was too dangerous for printers to handle and many aristocratic writers considered that printed books smacked too much of the market place. It is characteristic therefore of much Restoration poetry that it is found in loose manuscript sheets, in private commonplace books, and in some large volumes compiled by professional scribes. One of the finest of the latter sort was acquired by the Brotherton Collection in 1979. It is a substantial book of 463 pages, written in a series of calligraphic hands, and bound handsomely in contemporary red morocco stamped with gilt designs. It seems likely that a professional scribe began it in around 1680 and that subsequent hands, perhaps the owners', added further poems until about 1695. The volume, which was evidently first produced for a wealthy reader who wanted a collection of the most fashionable poetry, begins with Dryden's 'MacFlecknoe', the attack on Shadwell which circulated in manuscript between its composition in 1676 and authorised printing in 1684. The writer most frequently represented in the collection is the Earl of Rochester, whose songs and satires, often bawdy, were widely read in manuscript copies. Most of the remaining poems are topical satires on literary and political figures.

There are some 50 manuscript poetical miscellanies and commonplace books in the Brotherton Collection; there are others like that illustrated which are professional compilations, while more are the work of private individuals or families, selecting and preserving for their own interest. Some are valuable mainly for what they reveal of their compilers; their reading tastes are reflected and frequently their other activities, for the content may not be exclusively or conventionally literary. Other examples make significant contributions to the textual history of the poems included, or make unexpected attributions, or present new or unfamiliar poems amongst the better known. A couple here have illustrations and some list the contents of private libraries.

Our earliest commonplace book, dating from about 1600, was compiled by a Nicholas Hill, perhaps the philosopher of that name. The earliest with English verse, of about 1610, contains a poem, 'Of ambition', which it assigns to Fulke Greville and another by Sir Henry Wotton. An elegant, anonymous miscellany from the 1620s contains 54 mostly unrecorded poems, a dozen being directly associated with Hatfield and the Cecils; another less polished example appears to relate to Sir Daniel Fleming and a Salisbury School compilation of about 1700 has numerous poems by the elder Thomas Warton.

Most of the manuscripts of this kind date from 1680 to 1750, with a wide range of authors represented, Rochester, Marvell, Swift, and Pope appearing very frequently. An example deserving special mention is a fine Anglo-Irish miscellany of the 1730s containing poems by Swift and his circle, probably derived from other manuscript sources; some unpublished lines may be by Swift himself. Not all of these collections are in bound form; we have several accumulations of loose leaves of poems and other papers coming from single sources, individuals or families like the Luttrells.

Mac-Fleckno.

All human things are Subject to decay;
And, when Fate Summons, Monarchs must obey:
This **Fleckno** found; who, like **Augustus**, young
Was call'd to Empire, and had Govern'd long;
In Prose and Verse was own'd, without dispute,
Through all the Realm of Nonsence, absolute.
The aged Prince, now flourishing in peace,
And blest with Issue of a large increase,
Worn out with Bus'ness, did at length debate
To settle the Succession of the State;
And, pond'ring which of all his Sons were fit
To Reign, and wage immortal War with Wit:
Cry'd, 'Tis resolv'd; for Nature pleads that he
Should only Rule that most resembles Me:
Shadwell alone my perfect Image bears;
Mature in Dulness from his tender years:
Shadwell alone, of all my Sons, is he
Who stands confirm'd in full Stupidity;
The rest, to some faint meaning make pretence,
But **Shadwell** never deviates into Sence.

Some

9. WILLIAM SHAKESPEARE (1564–1616)

A Yorkshire Tragedie, *London, 1619.*

A Yorkshire Tragedy is a short but remarkable domestic tragedy written for the Jacobean stage. It dramatises the events leading up to the killing by Walter Calverley (of Calverley, near Leeds) of two of his three children on 23 April 1605. These murders caused a great stir at the time, and memory of them is still preserved in local legend. A prose pamphlet on the Calverley murders (*Two Most Unnaturall and Bloodie Murthers*) was entered in the Stationers' Register on 12 June 1605, less than two months after the crimes were committed and nearly two months before Calverley's trial and execution at York on 5 August 1605. The playwright's imaginative use of this pamphlet, which was his main source, is of considerable interest to students of Jacobean dramatic literature.

The external evidence for Shakespeare's authorship is impressive. The first quarto was entered by Thomas Pavier in the Stationers' Register on 2 May 1608 as the work of Shakespeare. The title-page of both quartos (this is the second) states that the play was written by W. Shakespeare, while the earlier adds that it was 'Acted by his Maiesties Players at the Globe'. The *Tragedy* was again attributed to Shakespeare in the transfers of copyright entered in the Stationers' Register on 4 August 1626 and 21 August 1683. Despite this strong external evidence, most twentieth-century scholars have refused to accept the play as Shakespeare's and have put forward a number of Shakespeare's contemporaries as possible authors. The likeliest of these is Thomas Middleton, whose authorship can be supported by objective linguistic evidence.

The earliest recorded performance of the play was given as part of a triple bill at the Boston Theatre, Boston, Mass., on 1 March 1847. Another noteworthy production took place at St Petersburg on 13 January 1895, when three short plays including *Yorkshirskaya tragediya* (translated by P. P. Gnedich) were performed. Anyone who has seen a stage revival of the *Tragedy* may agree with Baldwin Maxwell: 'Hastily written it probably was, but . . . its bare realism, and its fierce dramatic power . . . distinguish *A Yorkshire Tragedy* and set it among the few truly great domestic tragedies of its age'.

Another of Pavier's 1619 'Shakespeare' quartos is in the Collection, The First Part of the . . . History, of . . . Sir John Oldcastle, *falsely dated '1600'. These quartos have in fact many times the rarity of the 1623 first folio of Shakespeare's plays, of which we have two copies. Lord Brotherton acquired one from the American collector Theodore N. Vail, which was unknown to Sir Sidney Lee for his census of first folios; it has a few very minor repairs. The other copy, much less complete textually, is more celebrated, bearing the signatures of its former owners, William Congreve and Charles Killigrew, Master of the Revels. The Collection's second and fourth folios are both complete; the third lacks the seven newly added plays, but has early manuscript notes to* The Tempest.

The sole Elizabethan dramatic quarto is Henry Porter's The Two Angry Women of Abington, *1599, with a title-page variant unrecorded by Greg. From a little later, we have Jonson's* Volpone, *1607 (and his* Workes, *1616), John Day's* Lawe Trickes, *1608, indeterminate issues of Sir William Alexander's* Monarchick Tragedies, *and Robert Daborn's* A Christian Turn'd Turke, *1612.*

A
YORKSHIRE
TRAGEDIE.

Not so New, as Lamentable
and True.

Written by W. SHAKESPEARE.

Printed for *T. P.* 1619.

10. SIR WILLIAM KILLIGREW (1606–95)

Four New Playes, *London, 1666, and* The Imperial Tragedy, *London, 1669, with autograph manuscript emendations.*

This copy of *Four New Playes*, 1666, is extensively annotated by its author, Sir William Killigrew. His annotations also extend to a later play which has been bound in at the back of the volume. This, *The Imperial Tragedy*, was published anonymously in 1669. Commentators conjectured that Killigrew might be the author, but firm evidence was lacking. The annotations, and Killigrew's signature on the last page of *The Imperial Tragedy*, here confirm his authorship and suggest that he was preparing to reveal it in a new edition of his work.

Killigrew's annotations range from correction of printer's errors to large additions of dialogue and the inclusion of an Epilogue to *Selindra*. There is also his engaging admonition: 'Leave out these lines, tis not fitt to shew such great Monarks on the Stage, in such contempt!' (*The Imperial Tragedy*, p. 43).

The volume was purchased for the Brotherton Collection at a sale at Sotheby's on 13 June 1966. The only verifiable indication of previous ownership is the inscription made by punctures in the title-page which reads 'W.C./LIB'. This shows that the book once belonged to Alexander Thistlethwayte (1718–71) and that he may have intended it to be part of the large gift of books which he made to Winchester College in 1767. A similar, annotated, composite copy is in the Rosenbach Museum, Philadelphia. But the Brotherton volume is the more extensively corrected, and it more fully exemplifies the working methods of a seventeenth-century author.

After 1620 plays become progressively more numerous in the Collection. Some, like the Killigrew volume, are distinguished by manuscript additions; for example, amongst over 30 first editions of plays by James Shirley, there are an extensively annotated prompt copy for performance in the 1660s of Loves Crueltie, *1640, and* Six New Playes, *1653, with manuscript cast lists, one evidently recording a very early stage appearance by Nell Gwyn. A good run of first and early editions of Massinger's plays from* The Bond-man, *1624, onwards, includes a copy of* A New Way to Pay Old Debts *inscribed 'Alfred Tennyson from FL', the poet's note of a gift from Frederick Locker-Lampson. There are also many works by Fletcher, with and without Beaumont, and by others of whose work less is extant, like Ford, Marmion, May, and Nabbes, some in unusual copies.*

The collection of Dryden's plays contains some three-quarters of all the seventeenth-century editions, added to as opportunities arise. First editions of the major plays of his time, like Congreve's The Way of the World, *1700, Otway's* Venice Preserv'd, *1682, and Wycherley's* The Country Wife, *1675, are balanced by sole editions of some of the most obscure. Indeed, we have first and early editions of virtually all the plays of Mrs Behn, Congreve, Crowne, Etherege, Farquhar, Lee, Otway, Ravenscroft, Settle, Shadwell, Southerne, Tate, Vanbrugh, and Wycherley, authors varying greatly in their modern reputations. Several of these dramatists wrote well into the eighteenth century, when others prominent in the Collection are Mrs Centlivre, Fielding, Charles Johnson, Rowe, Theobald, and Gay, the several editions of whose* Beggar's Opera, *1728, etc., are accompanied by parodies and other derivative works.*

Enter Zeno, Longinus, Sebastianus, *as at a Banquet, drinking.*

Zeno. Brother, I drink a Kingdom to you here;
Longi. Long life, and health attend the Emperor.
Here's my Brothers health to you, *Sebastian.*
Sebast. Health, and highest happiness to *Cæsar.*
[*Here* Bacchus *is Drawn in a Chariot by* Tigers.
~~*Alexander and Antony.*~~

Sebast. See, *Bacchus* triumphs over Conquerors,
And looks as big as if he did disdain
Those Emperors, who now adorn his Train.
Zeno. Give me a full bowl: This *Falernian* Wine,
Than drunken *Bacchus* self, is more Divine.
Longi. Let's drink, till we become his Captives too,
And draw with *Antony*, and *Alexander.*
Zeno. Fill, *Anastasius*, let the cups go round:
Thou hast a sober face, so grave and wise,
As if thou did'st our jollities despise,
And mighty *Bacchus* powerful charms contemn.
Anast. What Mortal will contend? or who dares try
Great *Bacchus* force, after this Victory?

Leave out ~~these~~ lines
tis not ~~fitt to~~ shew such
great Monarks on
the stage in such
contempt. though my
Latin Author have
done it, I dislike it.
Th. K.

BACCHUS *his* SONG.

The Gods this noble Liquor made,
Mens melancholy hearts to aid;
To make you frolick, and set free
From cares and fears Captivity.
We, who with Liquid weapons fight,
T'imbrace, and hug, is our delight.

When I the strongest do subdue,
Fresh cups our friendship doe renew.
Ere we depart, the Victor still
Submits unto the Captives will;
And a new Battle by consent
Appointed is, in complement.

Chorus.

This Liquor of life invites us to sing,
This cheers the heart of the Begger, and King.
Then toss off your Bowls, and merrily tell,
How Bacchus *his slaves do Monarchs excel.*

11. WILLIAM SHAKESPEARE (1564–1616)

Poems, *London, 1640.*

Compared with the first collected edition of Shakespeare's plays, the first folio of 1623, this small volume, which constitutes the first collected edition of his poems, is unprepossessing in appearance. Though it survives in many fewer copies than the first folio, it is with apparent relish that commentators observe that, in John Hayward's words, it is 'not an uncommon book'. It is agreed to represent the result of a publisher's unauthorised opportunism, containing derivative texts lacking the integrity of the earlier separate editions from which it was compiled. Yet, despite all this, it remains, as recent book auction records powerfully attest, a keenly sought-after book, its desirability to collectors effortlessly surviving the contempt of editors and critics.

The book contains most of the sonnets — why eight from the first edition of 1609 were omitted is debatable — interspersed with poems from *The Passionate Pilgrim*, *The Lover's Complaint*, and *The Phoenix and the Turtle*, and poems by other poets including Jonson and Milton. The sonnets are reordered, given titles and slightly changed, making all appear to be addressed to a woman; later editors followed this approach until Malone's fine edition of 1790 reinstated the 1609 order and text, and speculation about 'Mr W.H.' and the poems' autobiographical significance could begin in earnest.

A brief note can hardly begin to survey the many volumes of English poetry of the seventeenth century and before in the Brotherton Collection. After items in Wotton's Speculum Christiani, *the earliest English printed poetry in the Collection is Pynson's Chaucer of 1526 (STC 5086, 5088 and 5096), alas rather imperfect. However, our second editions of Gower's* De Confessio Amantis, *1532, and of* Piers Plowman, *1550, are good copies, as are both 1596 volumes of Spenser's* The Faerie Queen*; we also have Spenser's* Complaints, *1591, and* Colin Clouts Come Home Againe, *the first issue of 1595.*

Amongst several works by Samuel Daniel we have his Poetical Essayes, *1599, and* The Civile Wares, *1609, with a marginal note possibly in the author's hand. Our* Virgidemiarum *by Joseph Hall (STC 12718 and 12719) has the scholar George Steevens's manuscript notes, while our copies of Nathaniel Baxter's* Sir Philip Sidney's Ourania, *1606, and of Suckling's* Aglaura, *1638, both bound in contemporary vellum, belonged to the Evelyn family. As well as individual works by John Taylor the water poet, such as* Heads of All Fashions, *1642, we have his* All the Workes, *1630, which includes his flyting with the Leeds-born poet William Fennor; we have the latter's* Fennors Descriptions, *1616, and* Pasquils Palinodia, *the second edition of 1634. Also from the 1630s, we have Walter Colman's rare* La Dance Machabre or Death's Duell, *probably 1633, Davenant's* Madagascar, *1638, with its 'remembrance' of Shakespeare, and most famous of all, John Donne's* Poems, *1633, a copy with the leaves 'The Printer to the Understanders' and 35 lines on page 273. Though we have only the fourth edition, 1635, of Herbert's* The Temple, *we have first editions of Crashaw's* Steps to the Temple, *1646, and Vaughan's* Olor Iscanus, *1651. Also from the 1640s are Lovelace's* Lucasta, *1649, and Cowley's* The Mistresse, *1647, evidently the true first edition.*

This Shadowe is renowned Shakespear's? Soule of th'age
The applause? delight? the wonder of the Stage.
Nature her selfe, was proud of his designes
And joy'd to weare the dressing of his lines;
The learned will Confess, his works are such,
As neither man, nor Muse, can prayse to much.
For ever live thy fame, the world to tell,
Thy like, no age, shall ever paralell.
W. M. sculpsit.

POEMS:

VVRITTEN BY WIL. SHAKE-SPEARE. Gent.

Printed at *London* by *Tho. Cotes*, and are to be sold by *Iohn Benson*, dwelling in S^t. *Dunstans* Church-yard. 1640.

12. ANDREW MARVELL (1621–78)

Miscellaneous Poems, *London, 1681.*

Lord Brotherton's first book-purchase (1922), encouraged by Mrs McGrigor Phillips after their unsuccessful bid for the Towneley Mysteries. As poems by one brought up in Hull, later its Member of Parliament, Marvell's verses, many glorifying his Fairfax family patrons and their Wharfe-side lands, were particularly appropriate in a local notable's library.

This posthumous collection, source of most of Marvell's poetry, may owe existence to its editor (Mary Palmer, his housekeeper) claiming for financial reasons marriage to Marvell. It omits post-Restoration satires attributed to him. The printer cancelled the major Cromwell poems (except in one, British Library, copy) and the pagination jumps 14 numbers.

Published from Marvell's autograph papers, the poems, English, Latin and Greek, may span 39 years from 1637 (Cambridge). Many were written whilst tutor to Mary, daughter to the retired General Thomas Fairfax, *circa* 1650–52; 'Bermudas' was apparently written (late 1653?) when Eton tutor lodging with John Oxenbridge, who had twice visited the islands.

Friend (and colleague under Cromwell) to Milton (and like him, a travelled man), Marvell's place is, rather, with the 'metaphysicals'. For public comment he prefers the heroic couplet, but for lyrical verse, chiefly 4–beat octosyllabic couplets. The words are often simple, the metre innocent (and not always artfully ridden), and there is observation of nature; but the mental ambience furnished *des forêts de symboles*, a network of classical allusions, of biblical and theological associations, of allegorical significances in everyday objects (as in contemporary emblem books), of Caroline masques, heroic theatre, mythologizing frontispieces. Glow-worms are 'country comets'; Captain Douglas burning alive on his ship is gilded with elegant 'conceits'. (Strange equipment against violent, revolutionary, intolerant, corrupt, plague-troubled times.) Many poems, including 'To his coy mistress' and the pastorals, reanimate classical and renaissance themes.

Though we must illustrate Marvell's work as the book which effectively began the Brotherton Collection, a more disinterested choice as the major volume of poetry of the later seventeenth century would be Milton's Paradise Lost, *1667. The priority of issues of its first edition remains debatable, but we welcome the view recently argued that the earliest is that with Milton's initials on the title-page, though dated '1668', for we have a copy; we have another issue of 1669,* Paradise Regain'd, *1671, and* Poems, &c., *1673 (first issue). Our several first editions of Milton's prose works include* Areopagitica, *1644.*

Later Dryden, who allegedly said of Milton 'This man cuts us all out', was pre-eminent. We have first and early editions of many of his separately printed poems beginning with Astræa Redux, *1660 (both states), and verse collections, translations and prologues. He has many contributions also in printed poetical miscellanies, a special interest of the Collection. Once again the abundance of poetry of the period present defies further description here, but good collections of work by Butler (and his imitators), Cotton, Denham, Oldham, Rochester, and Waller must be noted.*

MISCELLANEOUS

POEMS.

BY

ANDREW MARVELL, Esq;

Late Member of the Honourable House of Commons.

LONDON,

Printed for *Robert Boulter*, at the *Turks-Head* in *Cornhill*. M. DC. LXXXI.

13. JOHN DRYDEN (1631–1700)

Of Dramatick Poesie, an Essay, *London, 1668.*

Of Dramatic Poesie is the only formal critical work Dryden published separately, and the only criticism he ever revised. The modest seventy-two page booklet was probably published in late 1667 (dated 1668 on the title-page), but written nearly two years earlier, when Dryden fled the London Plague for the safety of Wiltshire in June 1666.

Dryden's pretence in his dedication to Lord Buckhurst that he came across 'this rude indigested' essay when 'lately reviewing my loose papers' is as ingenuous as the claim that its dialogue form means that 'all I have said is problematical'. In fact, the essay is deliberately written and carefully constructed, and of the four speakers, Neander (Dryden) is allowed the last word, even though the arguments are wide-ranging, the tone non-partisan. The essay is part of the European debate between the Ancients and the Moderns, particularly about whether English plays, like the French, should follow the classical 'precedent' in observing the three unities. Dryden's argument goes in favour of English variety and irregularity. Paradoxically, the vitality of English drama, with Jonson's *Silent Woman* as a key example, makes it the truer heir of classical drama than the narrower, but more 'correct', works by contemporary French dramatists. The essay is also part of the local controversy between Dryden and Sir Robert Howard, over the relative dramatic merits of blank verse and rhymed, Dryden's preference.

Of Dramatic Poesie is firmly nationalistic, an expression of the same cultural and aesthetic aspirations embodied in Wren's rebuilding of London after the Great Fire of 1666. Dryden demonstrates to his contemporaries and successors that the discussion of literature can be conducted through balanced, rationally argued debate, securely based on the analysis of critical terms and of specific examples.

For Dr Johnson, Dryden was 'the father of English criticism' but there were earlier progenitors. For Johnson's contemporary Thomas Warton, for example, Thomas Wilson's Arte of Rhetorike *(the 1567 edition is here) could be 'justly considered as the first book or system of criticism in our language'. Probably the first use of the term 'critic' in the modern literary sense is in Francis Bacon's* The Advancement of Learning, *1605 (our fine copy being bound in its original vellum).*

The Collection seeks to acquire critical works of the seventeenth and early eighteenth centuries, many, like the greater part of Dryden's criticism, appearing incidentally in volumes of drama or poetry. Thus verse surveys of poets by Drayton and by Suckling appear first in broader collections of their poems and Jonson's Discoveries *in his posthumous works of 1641; and the debate of Davenant and Hobbes occasioned by* Gondibert *was first published in England with the poem in 1651. More separate critical works appeared later, such as those we have relating to the Ancient-Modern quarrel of Temple, Bentley, and Wotton, ridiculed in Swift's* The Battle of the Books, *1704, and to the Collier controversy of the 1690s, including the contribution of John Dennis, arguably the first professional English critic. Dennis's dictatorial critical style — following Rymer and others before him — was deflated in Pope's* An Essay on Criticism, *1711, and superseded by the reader-centred approach of Addison's essays in* The Spectator, *1711–12, of which we have a full set of original issues.*

To the Right Honourable

CHARLES LORD BUCKHURST.

My Lord,

AS I was lately reviewing my loose Papers, amongst the rest I found this Essay, the writing of which in this rude and indigested manner wherein your Lordship now sees it, serv'd as an amusement to me in the Country, when the violence of the last Plague had driven me from the Town. Seeing then our Theaters shut up, I was engag'd in these kind of thoughts with the same delight with which men think upon their absent Mistresses: I confess I find many things in this discourse which I do not now approve; my judgment being a little alter'd since the writing of it, but whither for the better or the worse I know not: Neither indeed is it much material in an Essay, where all I have said is problematical. For the way of writing Playes in verse, which I have seem'd to favour, I have since that time laid the Practice of it aside, till I have more leisure, because I find it troublesome and slow. But I am no way alter'd from my opinion of it, at least with any reasons which

14. MATTHEW PRIOR (1664–1721)

A Letter to Monsieur Boileau Depreaux, *London, 1704.*

This poem was published within six weeks of the news of Marlborough's victory at Hochstadt (Blenheim) reaching England in August. Prior had in 1695 celebrated the recapture of Namur by writing a poem (also in the Brotherton Collection) in parodying response to Boileau's poem of 1692 celebrating the taking of Namur by Louis XIV. Thus the two poets conducted a sort of warfare in verse in keeping with the war between Britain and France. Samuel Johnson judged that 'The burlesque of Boileau's *Ode on Namur* has, in some parts, such airiness and levity as will always procure it readers, even among those who cannot compare it with the original. The *Epistle to Boileau* is not so happy'.

Prior had come to know Boileau while serving in 1699 as Secretary at the British Embassy in Paris during an interlude of peace. Boileau's *L'Art poétique*, in particular among his writings, had an important influence in Britain as elsewhere in Europe. The victory at Blenheim inspired many other poets, some still well-known and others who preferred anonymity at the time of publication and have deserved it since.

Bonamy Dobrée, Professor of English Literature at Leeds from 1936 to 1955 and a member of the Brotherton Collection Advisory Committee for 20 years, wrote of Prior in *English Literature in the Early Eighteenth Century* that poetry 'came naturally to him as a ready means of expression. He tells us in his *Essay upon Learning*, where he is speaking of the desire to write, "As to my own part I found this impulse very soon, and shall continue to feel it as long as I can think", and then, with engaging modesty, he describes how he came to abandon a literary career'.

Our knowledge of the nature, variety and availability of early eighteenth-century printed poetry has been enhanced enormously by D. F. Foxon's catalogue English Printed Verse, 1701–1750, *1975. Mr Foxon lists over 9,500 separately printed poems, unravelling much of their intricate history and bibliography and recording libraries where they may be found. The Brotherton Collection has over 1,000 of these poems, at least a quarter of which, including the Prior poem illustrated, are not actually noted as being at Leeds in the catalogue, usually because they have been acquired in the 20 years since the data for it were collected. We also have many of the collected editions of poetry which are less fully described in the catalogue.*

'Not in Foxon' has inevitably become the bookseller's proud claim for some rare items newly discovered; the Brotherton Collection's To Mr. ——— on his Essay upon Criticism, c. *1712, an early verse appreciation of Pope, is an example and we have others. Indeed, Mr Foxon's researches show that numerous works, of which the Collection has its share, seem to have survived only in unique, single copies, while others which he knew to have been printed but could not locate have more recently come to light, like our* The Aloe Tree, *1746. However, many Foxon items remain quite common, testimony to the great appetite for verse of early eighteenth-century readers.*

In one great Day on HOCHSTET'*s fatal Plain*
FRENCH *and* BAVARIANS *Twenty Thousand slain;*
Push'd thro' the DANUBE *to the Shoars of* STYX
Squadrons Eighteen, Battalions Twenty Six:
Officers Captive made and private Men,
Of these Twelve Hundred, of those Thousands Ten.
Tents, Ammunition, Colours, Carriages,
Cannons and Kettle-Drums—— sweet Numbers these.
AVE APOLLO!—— Sir——one Moment's Ease.
Tell me, is this to reckon or rehearse?
A Commissary's List, or Poet's Verse?

Why Faith, DEPREAUX, there's Sense in what you say,
I told you where my Difficulty lay;
He that can make the rough Recital chime,
Or bring the Sum of *Lewis'* Loss to Rhime,
May make Arithmetic and Epic meet,
And NEWTON'S Books in DRYDEN'S Stile repeat.

O BOILEAU, had it been APOLLO'S Will
That I had shar'd a Portion of thy Skill,
Had this poor Breast receiv'd the Heav'nly Beam,
And were my Numbers equal to my Theam,

To

15. ALEXANDER POPE (1688–1744)

The Dunciad, *London, 1728.*

On 18 May 1728 the London literary world was stirred into a flurry of activity by this modest duodecimo volume of under 60 pages: 'a Crowd of Authors besieg'd the Shop; Entreaties, Advices, Threats of Law, and Battery, nay Cries of Treason were all employ'd to hinder the coming out of the *Dunciad*: On the other Side, the Booksellers and Hawkers made as great Efforts to procure it'.

Alexander Pope's mock-heroic onslaught on the hacks, academics, media-men, producers, pornographers, and virtuosi of his day risked prosecution, and this rare first edition shows how he tried to cover his tracks. The Dublin imprint is false (perhaps to cast suspicion on some Irish wit — even his friend Swift?) and Anne Dodd, the nominal publisher, maintained her name had been used without her knowledge and consent. The frontispiece of the owl perched on an altar of 'dunce' volumes was soon cruelly parodied when Pope's enemies counter-attacked: they circulated a print of a Pope-headed monkey squatting on a pedestal piled high with his own works. Aware of legal dangers, Pope substituted dashes for individual names, allowing opportunists to publish various 'keys' to the poem's characters. All this worked so well that in 1729 he issued his grand *Dunciad Variorum* (180 pages) which named names and was grotesquely padded-out with mock-learned footnotes and layers of prefatory material and appendices. Pope's greatest joke was that within twelve months of this sly duodecimo publication the poem had swelled into a burlesque 'classic'.

The Collection has several more editions of The Dunciad, *besides those of 1728 and 1729, culminating in* The New Dunciad, *1742, incorporated in the reworked complete poem of 1743, in which Colley Cibber succeeded Theobald as king of the dunces. This was Pope's last major work; his first published appearance was in Tonson's* Poetical Miscellanies. The Sixth Part, *1709, which is also in the Collection, as are Pope's first separate publication,* An Essay on Criticism, *1711,* The Rape of the Lock *(in Lintot's 1712 miscellany and separately published, 1714), the rare* Court Ballad, *[1717], and many other works. We also have two books bearing Pope's signature, a small Elzevier Horace of 1629 and a volume of* Poems on affairs of state, *1697.*

There is much verse in the Collection of Pope's friends and major contemporaries. Swift claimed 'I had reason to put Mr. Pope *on writing the Poem, called the* Dunciad' *and his* On poetry. A rapsody, *1733, similarly savages Grub Street. Fellow Scriblerian John Gay's* Rural sports, *1713, is 'Inscribed to Mr.* Pope', *who helped to revise Gay's* The Fan, *1714. We have more works by them and Pope's other friends Parnell, Garth, Walsh, Congreve, who was dedicatee of Pope's* Iliad, *and Wycherley, our copy of whose* Miscellany Poems, *1704, has the author's presentation inscription to 'George Doddington Esqr'; another such inscription to Pope himself ('Ex dono authoris perquam amicissimi') is signed by James Thomson in his* Liberty, *1735. Samuel Johnson's first published work was a Latin translation, in Husbands's* Miscellany of Poems, *1731, of Pope's 'Messiah'; we have this and* London, *1738, which Pope much admired.*

DUBLIN;Printed;LONDON;Reprinted *for* A.Dodd

THE

DUNCIAD.

AN

Heroic Poem.

IN

THREE BOOKS.

DUBLIN, Printed, LONDON Reprinted for A. DODD. 1728.

16. JONATHAN SWIFT (1667–1745)

Autograph letter to Edward Harley, 9 February 1719/20.

More determined in seeking others' advancement than his own, Jonathan Swift was appointed Dean of St Patrick's Cathedral, Dublin, in April 1713 after years of hoping for preferment in England. In 1714, following the death of Queen Anne and the fall of his friend the Earl of Oxford, he resigned himself to an immediate future in Ireland and left for Dublin.

At first Swift's life in exile was secluded, his main occupation being his duties as Dean. To his acquaintance Knightley Chetwode he wrote in January 1715: 'I hear [my Chapter] think me a smart Dean; and that I am for doing good. My notion is, that if a man cannot mend the public he should mend old shoes . . . and therefore I endeavour in the little sphere I am placed to do all the good it is capable of'. Swift sought to improve the Cathedral in various ways, taking a special interest in its choir and music as we see in this letter to Oxford's brother; in it Swift brilliantly combines comment on his predecessors, politicians' appointments and poets — and on himself, though if he truly did 'understand Musick like a Muscovite', as he puts it, he had an excuse in his chronic bouts of deafness.

Swift's Dublin correspondence kept alive not only his friendships but his skill as a writer: 'I know very well that you can write a good letter, if you have a mind to it', wrote Matthew Prior to him in April 1721. By that time, the writing was becoming more public again in a series of published pamphlets and Swift had started *Gulliver's Travels*, the finished manuscript of which he brought with him on his eventual return to London in 1726.

We have regularly acquired works of prose satire from the seventeenth and early eighteenth centuries, though less commonly than verse satires and rarely in manuscript form. Several of the more celebrated works are by Swift, of whom we have many first editions, including A Tale of a Tub, *1704, and* Gulliver's Travels, *1726, Teerink's 'B' issue with, most appropriately, a label inside reading 'John Brotherton . . . bindeth all Sorts of Books'. There are also numerous imitations and parodies of Swift.*

There are several satires in the Collection by Dr John Arbuthnot, Swift's friend who incidentally advised him on his choir at St Patrick's. An Arbuthnot adversary Dr John Woodward is also the butt of satires here by Richard Mead and by William Wagstaffe, and there are many other examples of topics and persons, like Sacheverell and Walpole, being satirised by more than one author. In general we do not collect novels, but we have some satirical romans à clef *by Mrs Manley and others, and several minor satirical prose pieces by Henry Fielding.*

From earlier periods the prolific Thomas Brown of Shifnal is particularly well represented in prose, as in verse, and we have various satirical works by Richard Brathwaite, including The Arcadian princesse, *1635,* Panthalia, *1659,* The chimney's scuffle, *1662, and* Whimzies, *1631, a book of characters with strong satiric elements. Other examples of character writing present include works by Cleveland and Halifax and the striking* A Strange Metamorphosis of Man, *1634, which may also be by Brathwaite.*

famous Memory, that the Race of People called Gentlemen Lovers of Musick, tell me I must be very carefull in supplying two Vacancyes, which I have been two Years endeavoring to do. For you are to understand, that in disposing these Musicall Employments I determine to act directly contrary to Ministers of State, by giving them to those who best deserve. If you had recommended a Person to me for a Church-Living in my Gift, I would be less curious; because an indifferent Parson may do well enough, if he be honest, but Singers like their brothers the Poets must be very good, or they are good for Nothing. I wish my Lord Oxford had writ to me on this Subject that I might have had the Pleasure of refusing him in direct Terms.

If you will order Mr Lovelace to enquire for one Rosingrave my Organist now in London, and approve his Skill to him; on his Report I shall be ready to accept Lovelace: which is the Short of the Matter that I have made so many words of, in revenge for your saying nothing of what I would desire to know: and I must desire you to put my Lord Oxford in mind of sending me his Picture, for it is just eight Years last Tuesday since he promised me. If you had but said one Syllable of my Sister Harriette I could have pardoned you.

Pray believe that there is no man who can possibly have a greater Respect for You and Your Family than My Self, Nothing but a Scurvy State of Health could have hindred me from the Happiness of once more seeing you all.

I am

with great Respect

Sr Your most obedient

and most humble Servt

J: Swift

17. VOLTAIRE (1694–1778)

Letters concerning the English Nation, *translated from the French by John Lockman, London, 1733.*

This is a translation famous for having appeared in print before its French original. In April 1733, Voltaire was smarting from the *furore* raised by his *Temple du Goût* and he did not dare publish his *Lettres Philosophiques* in France. He therefore asked his friend Thieriot to organise this English version and present it as a private correspondence. If we can believe Voltaire, 3,000 copies were soon run off, although publication was only announced in the *Gentleman's Magazine* of August. The English text is by John Lockman, a journalist and translator of many French works. He had already produced a remarkably anti-French and anti-Catholic version of *La Henriade*. According to the Abbé Prévost, in the first volume of *Le Pour et Contre*, 1733, Lockman was not entirely faithful to Voltaire's original manuscript, and the English text also differs from the first French edition of 1734 for other reasons. Most noticeably, it lacks the final letter 25, in which Voltaire leaves England and attacks Pascal.

Voltaire hoped that even the most serious letters would 'be found entertaining' and one can certainly sense the witty manner that was to give lasting fame to *Candide*. A foreigner flits from one subject to another and makes telling ingenuous remarks. Here Voltaire surveys through analogy the preoccupations of the Enlightenment. Through English attitudes to religion, philosophy, government, and the arts, Voltaire pleads amusingly for individual freedom. To prove his point, the French version was naturally banned.

The Brotherton Collection has many major works of translation into English of the seventeenth and early eighteenth centuries. Just before this period, Arthur Golding was perhaps the first who could be considered a professional translator; we have his Trogus Pompeius, 'corrected', 1570, and Solinus, 1587. A little later Philemon Holland earned the description in Fuller's Worthies *'the translator generall of his age' and we have all his massive classical translations published from 1600 to 1632; in the Brotherton Collection, as in the imagined library in Pope's* Dunciad, *'the groaning shelves Philemon bends'. More celebrated individual classical translations here include Gavin Douglas's Scots* Aeneid, *1553; from Ovid, Marlowe's* Elegies *(STC 18932) and Sandys's* Metamorphoses, *1626; and most famous of all, Chapman's Homer (*The Whole Works, *1616). Even the exacting Ben Jonson, whose own translation of Horace's* Ars Poetica, *1640, we have, acknowledged the quality of Chapman's work, though greater reservations were held by Dryden and Pope, whose major translations are all here. Amongst a number of manuscript translations present are one from Seneca by Sir Edward Dering (died 1689) and a version of Cicero's* De Amicitia, *c. 1700, said once to have belonged to Shelley.*

We also have translations on many subjects from modern languages. From the French, for example, there are Florio's fine Essayes *of Montaigne, 1603, and John Evelyn's translation of Fréart's* A Parallel of the Antient Architecture with the Modern, *1664, with Evelyn's autograph presentation inscription to John Beale. Translations from the Italian include the first versions of Machiavelli in English, made by Edward Dacres, and from the Spanish we have all the translations of* Don Quixote *from Shelton's to Jarvis's.*

LETTERS

CONCERNING THE

ENGLISH NATION.

BY

Mr. DE VOLTAIRE.

LONDON,
Printed for C. DAVIS in *Pater-Noster-Row*,
and A. LYON in *Russel-Street*, *Covent-Garden*.
MDCCXXXIII.

18. THOMAS GRAY (1716–71)

Luna est habitabilis, *[Cambridge], [1737].*

When Thomas Gray went up from Eton to Cambridge, in October 1734, he had already written some Latin verse exercises. His talents must then have attracted attention for at the end of 1736 he wrote to his friend Horace Walpole 'the Moderatour has asked me to make the Tripos-Verses this year', these being Latin verses written by undergraduates for distribution with the annual lists of successful Tripos candidates.

The poem which Gray prepared for the Comitia Posteriora of mid-March 1737 was entitled *Luna est habitabilis*, a fantasy which has been claimed as early science fiction. The poet, gazing at the moon through a telescope, speculates that it is inhabited by people who in turn observe the earth; he predicts travel to and from the moon, with England colonising it and dominating the skies as she rules the seas.

The earliest printing of the poem available to Gray's recent editors has been that in *Musae Etonienses*, 1755, an anthology of Etonian verse compiled by John Prinsep; the whereabouts of a copy of the 1737 printing has been unknown since one was sold at auction in 1854, until the Brotherton Collection acquired this copy in 1984. It is printed on one side only of a long leaf like a galley proof, now cut in two, and its origins are shown by the concluding catchwords '*In Comitiis Posterior*'. Prinsep's version is seen to be substantially accurate, though the full title includes the verb and it is confirmed that he misread words in lines 21, 44, and 73.

Besides the Gray poem illustrated, there are three manuscript fragments in his autograph here, including some journal entries for April 1763. Generally, the Collection's interests in the second half of the eighteenth century are less extensive than in the first, but there are some other notable items. Poets particularly well represented are Smart and Charles Churchill, and we have unpublished manuscript collections of verse and dramatic pieces by the brothers Theodosius and Frederick Forrest; Theodosius was solicitor to Covent Garden Theatre and a friend of Garrick, whose own printed plays are numerous here.

Most of the prose works present are not in major editions, but we have good copies of Boswell's Johnson, *1791, and of* Tristram Shandy, *1766, with the two York-printed volumes and the later ones with Sterne's authenticating signatures. There are several examples of Richardson's printing and an engaging autograph letter from him to Miss Highmore, 20 July 1750.*

A number of items reflect Mrs McGrigor Phillips's love of Burns. We have her copy of the Kilmarnock edition of Poems, Chiefly in the Scottish Dialect, *1786, five volumes of* The Scots Musical Museum, *1787–92, and the suppressed* Letters Addressed to Clarinda, *1802. Still more striking are a delicately-made ring engraved 'Robt. Burns to Bonnie Jean 1786', evidently presented to Jean Armour, and two silhouette portraits by John Miers, one of the poet's mother Agnes and the other of Burns himself, inscribed 'Kilmarnock 1787' and with the name of John Cotterell to whom it seems to have been given.*

Luna eſt habitabilis.

DUM nox rorantes non incomitata per auras
Urget equos, tacitoque inducit ſidera lapſu:
Ultima, ſed nulli ſoror inficianda ſororum,
Huç mihi, Muſa: tibi patet alti janua cœli,
Aſtra vides, nec te numeri, nec nomina fallunt.
Huc mihi, Diva, veni: dulce eſt per aperta ſerena
Vere frui liquido, campoque errare ſilenti;
Vere frui dulce eſt; modo tu dignata petentem
Sis comes, & mecum gelidâ ſpatiere ſub umbrâ.
Scilicet hos orbes, cœli hæc decora alta putandum eſt,
Noctis opes, nobis tantum lucere; virûmque
Oſtentari oculis, noſtræ laquearia terræ,
Ingentes ſcenas, vaſtique aulæa theatri?
Oh! quis me pennis æthræ ſuper ardua ſiſtet
Mirantem, propiúſque dabit convexa tueri;
Teque adeo, undè fluens reficit lux mollior arva,
Pallidiorque dies, triſtes ſolata tenebras?
Sic ego, ſubridens Dea ſic ingreſſa viciſſim:
Non pennis opus hìc, ſupera ut ſimul illa petamus:
Diſce puer potiùs cœlo deducere Lunam;
Neu crede ad magicas te invitum accingier artes,
Theſſalicoſve modos: ipſam deſcendere Phœben
Conſpicies, novus Endymion; ſeque offeret ultrò
Viſa tibi ante oculos, & notâ major imago.
Quin tete admoveas (tumuli ſuper aggere ſpectas
Compoſitum) tubulo; ſimul imum invade canalem
Sic intentâ acie, cœli ſimùl alta pateſcent
Atria; jamque, auſus Lunaria viſere regna,
Ingrediére ſolo, & caput inter nubila condes.
Ecce autem! vitri ſe in vertice ſiſtere Phœben
Cernis, & Oceanum, & crêbris Freta conſita terris:
Panditur *ille* atram faciem caligine condens
Sublustri, refugitque oculos, fallitque tuentem;
Integram Solis lucem quippè haurit aperto
Fluctu avidus radiorum, & longos imbibit ignes:
Verùm *his*, quæ, maculis variata nitentibus, auro
Cærula diſcernunt, celſo ſeſe inſula dorſo
Plurima protrudit, prætentaque littora ſaxis;
Liberior datur his quoniàm natura, minúſque
Lumen depaſcunt liquidum; ſed tela diei
Detorquent, retróque docent ſe vertere flammas.
Hinc longos videas tractus, terraſque jacentes
Ordine candenti, & claros ſe attollere montes;
Montes, queîs Rhodope aſſurgat, quibus Oſſa nivali
Vertice: tum ſcopulis infrà pendentibus antra
Nigreſcunt clivorum umbrâ, nemorumque tenebris.
Non rores illî, aut deſunt ſua nubila mundo;
Non frigus gelidum, atque herbis gratiſſimus imber:
His quoque nota ardet picto Thaumantias arcu,
Os roſeum Auroræ, propriique crepuſcula cœli.
Et dubitas tantum certis cultoribus orbem
Deſtitui? exercent agros, ſua mænia condunt
Hi quoque, vel Martem invadunt, curantque triumphos
Victores: ſunt hic etiam ſua præmia laudi;
His metus, atque amor, & mentem mortalia tangunt.
Quin, uti nos oculis jam nunc juvat ire per arva,
Lucenteſque plagas Lunæ, pontumque profundum:
Idem illos etiàm ardor agit, cum ſe aureus effert
Sub ſudum globus, & Terrarum ingentior orbis;
Scilicet omne æquor tum luſtrant, ſcilicet omnem
Tellurem, genteſque polo ſub utroque jacentes:
Et quidam æſtivi indefeſſus ad ætheris ignes
Pervigilat, noctem exercens, cœlumque fatigat;
Jam Galli apparent, jam ſe Germania latè
Tollit, & albeſcens pater Apenninus ad auras:
Jam tandem in Borean, en! parvulus Anglia nævus
(Quanquàm aliis longè fulgentior) extulit oras:
Formoſum extemplò lumen, maculamque nitentem
Inviſunt crebri Proceres, ſerúmque tuendo
Hærent, certatímque ſuo cognomine ſignant:
Forſitan & Lunæ longinquus in orbe Tyrannus
Se dominum vocat, & noſtrâ ſe jactat in aulâ.
Terras poſſim alias propiori Sole calentes
Narrare; atque alias, jubaris queîs parcior uſus,
Lunarum chorus, & tenuis penuria Phœbi:
Nî, meditans eadem hæc audaci evolvere cantu,
Jàm pulſet citharam Soror, & præludia tentet.
Non tamen has proprias laudes, nec facta ſilebo
Jampridèm in fatis, patriæque oracula famæ.
Tempus erit, ſursùm totos contendere cœtus
Quo cernes longo excurſu, primoſque colonos
Migrare in lunam, & notos mutare Penates:
Dum ſtupet obtutu tacito vetus incola, longéque
Inſolitas explorat aves, claſſemque volantem.
Ut quondàm ignotum marmor, campoſque natantes
Tranavit Zephyros viſens, nova regna, Columbus;
Litora mirantur circùm, mirantur & undæ
Incluſas acies ferro, turmaſque biformes,
Monſtraque fœta armis, & non imitabile fulmen.
Fœdera mox icta, & gemini commercia mundi,
Agminaque aſſueto glomerata ſub æthere cerno.
Anglia, quæ pelagi jamdudùm torquet habenas,
Exercetque frequens ventos, atque imperat undæ;
Aëris attollet faſces, vetereſque triumphos
Hùc etiam feret, & victis dominabitur auris.

Grey

In Comitiis Poſterior

19. GEORGE FOX (1624–91), JOHN STUBBS, and BENJAMIN FURLY

A Battle-door for Teachers & Professors to Learn Singular & Plural, *London, 1660.*

Probably the most remarkable book of the early years of Quakerism is the *Battle-door*, an unimpressive, erratically-printed small folio volume, with many curious founts of type to illustrate its theme in more than thirty languages. Some pages, like that reproduced, are printed within a ruled frame shaped like a horn-book, or battledore.

The book demonstrates that grammatical principles in ancient and modern languages require singular address to one person. The idea and driving force came from Fox; the learning from Stubbs and Furly. George Fox in his *Journal*, beginning his preaching journeys in 1648, says 'I was required to Thee and Thou all men and women, without any respect to rich or poor, great or small'. This was one facet of the Quaker drive for plainness and simplicity. Polite language was adopting plural forms — 'by way of flattery' as William Penn says. Singular forms were restricted to addressing inferiors or delivering insults, as Coke to Raleigh at his trial, 'I thou thee, thou traitor', though the language of the Bible, school books and customary North Country speech still accepted the singular as grammatically correct.

Quakers presented copies to dignitaries in church and state. The King, according to Fox's *Journal*, was impressed, Archbishop Juxon so astonished at it that he was at a loss for words. 'It so confounded people that few after were so rugged against us for saying "thee" and "thou" to a single person'.

We have a representative selection of seventeenth- and eighteenth-century dictionaries and grammars. Demand for such works in the period before Johnson's dictionary was great. Thus the Collection has four editions of Henry Cockeram's English Dictionarie, *1631–55, the first to use this title, four also of Thomas Blount's* Glossographia *including the first, 1656, and six editions from the first of 1676 of Elisha Coles's dictionary. Descendants of these works appeared into the next century, joined then by the notable dictionaries of John Kersey, 1708, and Nathaniel Bailey, 1721. Bailey's work was plagiarised by Defoe's son for a dictionary of 1735 and referred to by Dr Johnson when engaged in the single-handed harmless drudgery of preparing his great* Dictionary *of 1755. All these are here.*

We also have a variety of multi-lingual and bi-lingual dictionaries, including Florio's Queen Anna's New World of Words, *1611, a copy of Miège's* Great French Dictionary, *1687–88, once owned by Thomas Rawlinson, and the* Lexicon Tetraglotton, *1659–60, by Jonson's friend James Howell. There are also various specialised dictionaries in the Collection, such as those for ladies (1694), gentlemen (1705), and sportsmen (1735); commonest are those of legal terms, the earliest of which is Cowell's* Interpreter, *1607, our copy having belonged to Robert Nares, the philologist.*

Many grammars, but not the Battle-door, *also went through many editions in this period. We have, for example, over 30 editions of works published between 1651 and 1775 written for schools by Charles Hoole, a master of Rotherham School. Our manuscript grammar of some 200 pages,* c. *1710, by Captain John Stevens, the translator, seems never to have been published.*

THE SYRIACK BATTLE-DOOR.

First see the Letters.

In the end.		In the middle.	In the beginning of a word.	
ܐ	ܐ	ܐ	ܐ	A
ܒ	ܒ	ܒ	ܒ	B, *or* Bh, *or* u
ܓ	ܓ	ܓ	ܓ	G, *or* Gh
ܕ	ܕ	ܕ	ܕ	D, *or* Dh
ܗ	ܗ	ܗ	ܗ	H
ܘ	ܘ	ܘ	ܘ	V,u
ܙ	ܙ	ܙ	ܙ	Z
ܚ	ܚ	ܚ	ܚ	Hh, Ch
ܛ	ܛ	ܛ	ܛ	T, tt
ܝ	ܝ	ܝ	ܝ	J i y
ܟ	ܟ	ܟ	ܟ	K, c, *or* Ch
ܠ	ܠ	ܠ	ܠ	L
ܡ	ܡ	ܡ	ܡ	M
ܢ	ܢ	ܢ	ܢ	N
ܣ	ܣ	ܣ	ܣ	S
ܥ	ܥ	ܥ	ܥ	Aa, *or* Oo
ܦ	ܦ	ܦ	ܦ	P,Ph, *or* F
ܨ	ܨ	ܨ	ܨ	Tſ,tz,z, ſſ
ܩ	ܩ	ܩ	ܩ	Q, *or* K
ܪ	ܪ	ܪ	ܪ	R
ܫ	ܫ	ܫ	ܫ	Sh, Sch
ܬ	ܬ	ܬ	ܬ	Th, *or* t

This letter ܥ is not expreſſed in ſound in the Battle-Door, becauſe the pronunciation of it is unknown to the Grammarians themſelves,

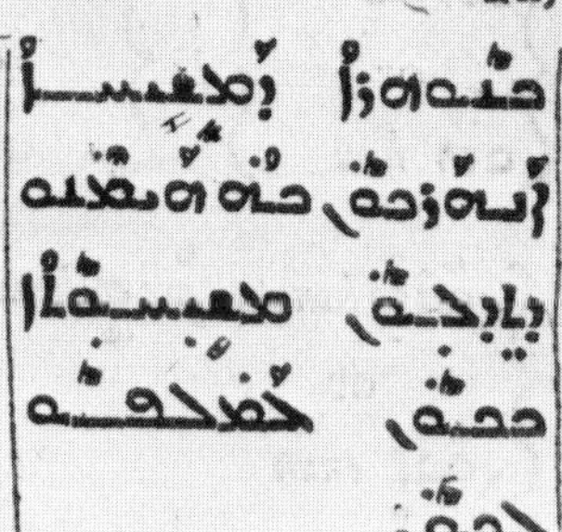

Geo. Fox.

20. AN ABSTRACT OF A VOYAGE FROM ENGLAND TO THE MEDITERANIAN

Anonymous manuscript journal, 1694–96.

This is the journal of an anonymous victualler in the service of the Royal Navy, sent to the Mediterranean with food for the Anglo-Dutch fleet during the final years of the Nine Years War (1688–97). This war was a pivotal period in the long-term development of British naval policy, witnessing two historic firsts: the main British fleet entered the Mediterranean, and the fleet wintered in a foreign port (Cadiz). This appears to be the only detailed record of a victualler of this period to survive and is thus one of the few sources of information available about the day-to-day operations of the victualling service at sea.

The logistics of supplying over 20,000 men with fresh victuals were formidable. Britain did not have a base of her own in the Mediterranean, and the Spanish were unreliable, so most supplies had to be sent 1100 miles from Britain, the remainder being sought in the war-ravaged Spanish countryside. In recording each detail of his work the victualler reveals much of interest to the modern historian: weights, measures and coinage in the various ports; where to buy good, cheap wines; the price of foodstuffs; how English merchants could circumvent the Spanish prohibition on trade to the West Indies; imports to and exports from Cadiz; and more.

Unfortunately little is known of the author other than that he was one of two clerks assisting the Victualling Commissioner in charge of the expedition, but the journal offers much indirect evidence of his personality. Always 'anxious not to waste any time', he conscientiously collected and recorded information about the places of historic interest he visited in Spain and his impressions of the people he encountered. He also knew how to tell a good story, enlivening his account with anecdotes about Pedro the Cruel, the red-light district of Cagliari, and many others.

Thus the journal enables us to understand better the operation of the British Navy at a crucial point in its history and to recapture some of the texture as well as the structure of seventeenth-century life.

The earliest item in the small but interesting group of travel manuscripts of the seventeenth and eighteenth centuries in the Collection is a journal of travel through Western Europe in 1611–12, probably by Sir Charles Somerset, son of the 4th Earl of Worcester. Another manuscript is Sir William Trumbull's lively diary of travel in Italy and France, March 1664 to May 1665; a companion, Sir Thomas Browne's son Edward, described part of the same tour in the second edition of his Travels, *1685. The brief 'A journall of my voiage into Holland to fetch ye Prince of Orange 7th October 1670' is ascribed to Sir Edward Turnour the elder; the Prince's entertainment of the author's party led by the Earl of Ossory is described, with the sardonic comment 'I cant say much for the dinner for twas very ordinary'. A longer, more enthusiastic account of Holland appears in an anonymous gentleman's manuscript 'Travells into Holland &c', 1687. Rather later is George Aptall's record of his hectic misadventures as a merchant captain in the Mediterranean, 1711–15.*

A Draught of ye Bay of Callarry from Cape Pulo to ye West to Cape Carbonero on ye East wch is about Twenty mile over accordg to the Dimension I took as on ye Other Side

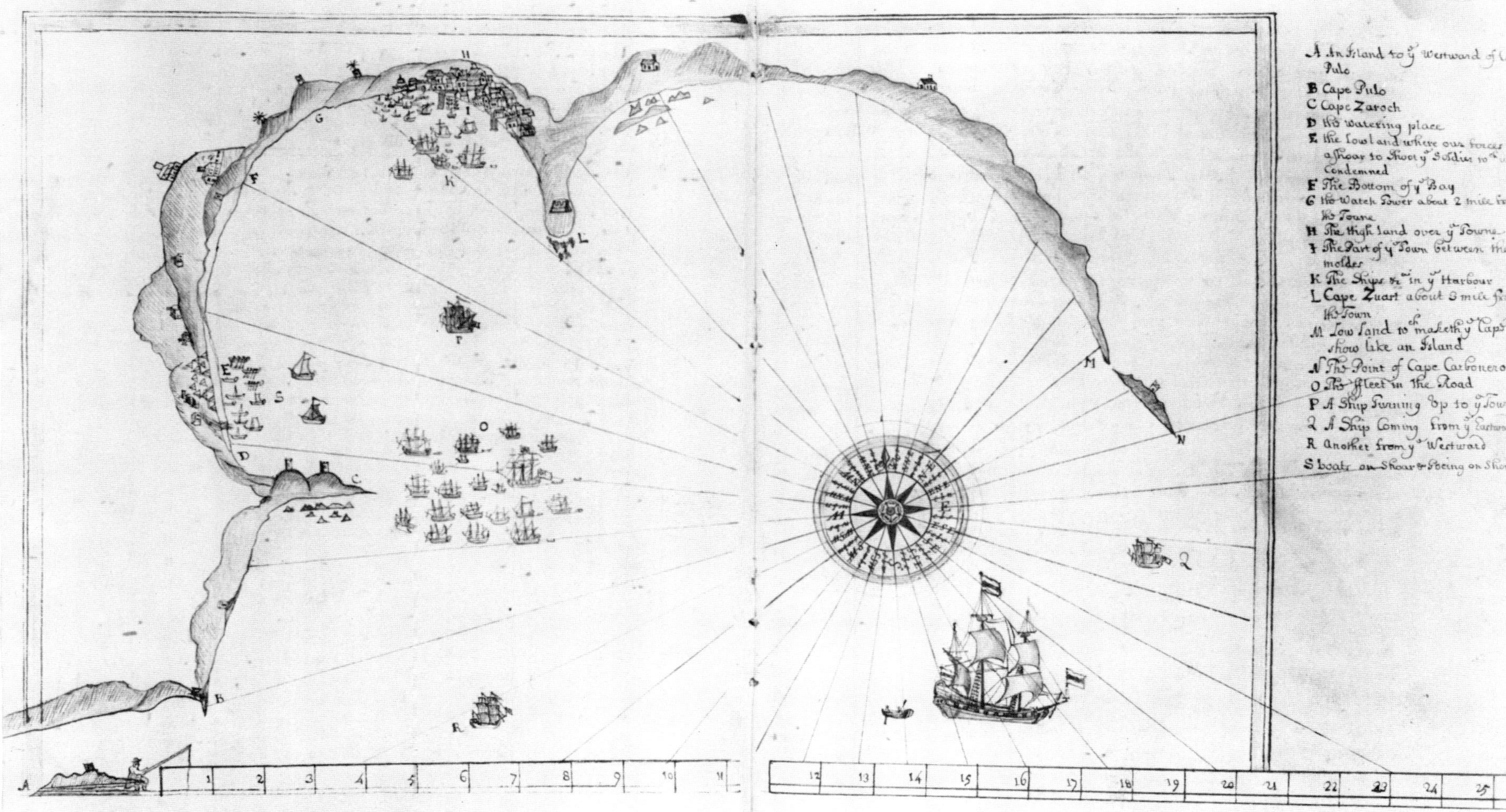

A Description of the Letters in this Draught

A An Island to ye Westward of Cape Pulo
B Cape Pulo
C Cape Zaroch
D the watering place
E the Low land where our forces was ashoar to Shoot ye Soldier wch was Condemned
F The Bottom of ye Bay
G the Watch Tower about 2 mile from the Towne
H The high land over ye Towne
I The Part of ye Town between the moldes
K The Ships &c in ye Harbour
L Cape Zuart about 3 mile from the Town
M Low land wch maketh ye Cape show like an Island
N The Point of Cape Carbonero
O The ffleet in the Road
P A Ship Turning Up to ye Town
Q A Ship Coming from ye Eastward
R Another from ye Westward
S boats on Shoar & being on Shore

21. JERONYMO LOBO (1596?–1678)

A Voyage to Abyssinia, *translated from the French version of J. Legrand by Samuel Johnson, London, 1735, with autograph manuscript notes by Thomas Percy, Bishop of Dromore.*

The editor and scholar Thomas Percy (1729–1811) met James Bruce in the summer of 1774 at Alnwick Castle, where, he records, Bruce 'gave a full Relation of his Travels into Abyssinia' which made 'so strong an impression' on Percy that 'some time after', on acquiring this book, he 'wrote them down — at the Beginning, End & Margins'. Bruce was then at the height of his fame, having just returned from Abyssinia via the courts and salons of Italy, France, and London, with tales of barbaric customs which amazed his contemporaries. Percy was here able to record at first hand some of these tales, which Bruce himself did not relate in print until some sixteen years later, when he published his *Travels to discover the source of the Nile*, 5 vols., 1790. By that time Bruce had been unfairly discredited and he was more commonly regarded as a figure of fun than of authority, a view which Percy himself came to share since he then returned to his notes in this book, made a few deletions to obscure some of the traces of his earlier credulity and remarked 'It may be judged how much I was surprized to find in his Book so very different an Account of his Travels'.

Percy's notes occupy altogether eleven sides of flyleaves and blank pages in the volume, as well as margins of more than fifty pages of the printed text. It is thus one of the most heavily annotated volumes in his library, the greater part of which is now preserved at the Queen's University, Belfast.

Books concerned with travels in Europe and through other countries bordering on the Mediterranean published during the seventeenth century and the first half of the eighteenth are particularly sought for the Collection. Together with more general accounts of voyages and travels, there are some 300 such works present, many of them listed in two handlists.

Our copy of Richard Hakluyt's Voyages, *1599–1600, is of the second edition, but at the end of the first volume it still has the seven suppressed leaves of the voyage to Cadiz. Purchas's* Pilgrimes, *1625, is the first edition, all volumes in unusually good condition, as is his* Pilgrimage, *1626.* Coryats crudities, *1611, is also a fine complete copy with the plates uncropped, accompanied by an early issue of* Coryats crambe, *1611, with the Boies Penrose bookplates which are also to be seen here in copies of works by Treswell, Dallington, Charles Robson and, unexpectedly linking bad weather in Yorkshire with Maltese topography,* Newes from Babylon, *1637; there are several more intriguing news books and other early authors well represented are Brinckmair, Lewkenor, Lithgow, Fynes Moryson, George Sandys, and Wadsworth.*

Later sets of travels and voyages include those of Le Bruyn, Tavernier, Hacke, Astley, Osborne, the Churchills and, later still, Cook's (the eight volumes of the three voyages, 1773–85) and Ayton's Voyage round Great Britain, *1814–25.*

The CONTENTS.

Mr. Bruce said, that when he was exploring the internal Parts of the ancient Libya, he constantly met with roving tribes of Nomades who still answered the Description given of them by Virgil. viz. Geo. III. (339.

THE END.

Quid tibi Pastores Libyæ, quid pascua versu
Prosequar, et raris habitata mapalia tectis?
Sæpe diem noctemque & totum ex ordine mensem
Pascitur, itque pecus longa in deserta sine ullis
Hospitiis: tantum campi jacet. Omnia secum
Armentarius Afer agit; tectumque, laremque,
Armaque, Amyclæumque canem, Cressamque pharetram.

The substance of what I heard Mr. Bruce relate in 1774. Thos. Percy

In 1773 or 1774 returned to Europe James Bruce Esq. who, I believe, had been Consul or Vice-Consul, in one of the Barbary States, and having some reason to be displeased with his Situation, left it & spent several years in penetrating into different Parts of Africa: at first he explored the Ruins of the old Roman Towns, in what was the Ancient Numidia & Mauritania: & being a nice Draughtsman, took Sketches of the fine Remains of elegant Buildings; wch stillars found there, tho' utterly unknown to common Antiquaries & Virtuosi, & wch according to him, have suffered less than those in Italy, Greece, or Asia. Of these he afterwards made most finished Drawings, wch at present are in possession of K. George III on whom he had demands for 6000.ll This Money was paid him, & he made his Majesty a present of his fine Drawings, wch are allowed to be of the first rate merit.

22. BERNARD MANDEVILLE (1670?–1723)

An Enquiry into the Causes of the Frequent Executions at Tyburn, *London, 1725.*

Bernard Mandeville was a Dutch physician practising in London and his high intelligence, moral concern, and rational scepticism inform and animate his accounts of London life and the English scene. His most famous work is *The Fable of the Bees*, 1714–29; among his pamphlets *A Modest Defence of Public Stews*, 1724, is in the same genre as the *Enquiry*.

The *Enquiry* was first published as a series of letters to *The British Journal* beginning 27 February 1725, a few days before the arrest of Jonathan Wild, celebrated thief-taker and notorious dealer in stolen property. Mandeville's first argument in the *Enquiry* is against honest citizens who connived at felony by buying back stolen goods, so defeating the Act of 1718 aimed at 'receivers'. The importance of the *Enquiry* today is in its contemporary, vivid, almost cinematic account of Newgate and of execution day at Tyburn. This is Hogarth in uncompromising and sharply etched prose, as plainly alive as the best work of a great contemporary, Defoe.

Mandeville's alternative to the violent drunken circus at Tyburn and to the mob adulation of such thieves as 'Sixteen String Jack' Rann (*The Beggar's Opera* was first presented in 1728) was to impose an extreme rigour on the condemned criminal. Such should be held in solitary confinement on bread and water only and under formal religious instruction, so that, on delivery to the gallows, the people would see 'a pale and frightened man' and would be depressed and silenced by his miserable state. This would be a true moral warning against crime. He suggests other 'reforms' concerned with transportation and the exchange of condemned men for prisoners held as slaves by pirates, but he is clearly less concerned with pity for the prisoner than with the enforcement of the authority and dignity of the law. He precedes the main movement for penal reform derived from the Enlightenment (e.g. Beccaria, 1748) and of which the chief English example was to be Fielding's famous *An Enquiry into the Causes of the Late Increase of Robbers, &c*, 1751 (also in the Brotherton Collection).

The Collection has a distinct group of some 300 printed volumes directly concerned with social, political and economic affairs published from about 1600 to 1750. Most unusual is a copy of Samuel Pepys's Memoires Relating to the State of the Royal Navy of England, *1690, which has manuscript corrections throughout, possibly in Pepys's own hand, and the author's presentation inscription dated 1693 to 'E. Smith', probably Pepys's relative and father of his godchild. Numerous works by and about Hobbes include an edition of* Leviathan *dated 1651, the year in which the controversial work first appeared, but probably published as late as 1680, taking advantage of popular interest in the year after Hobbes's death. Roger Coke, Defoe, Locke (*Some Considerations of the Consequences of the Lowering of Interest, *1692, and* Further Considerations, *1695), and Sir William Petty are well represented.*

A separate section contains hundreds of seventeenth-century political pamphlets; most relate to the Civil War and its aftermath, but there is much later by and about L'Estrange. A series of editions of Eikon Basilike *includes copies presented by the work's bibliographer F. F. Madan.*

AN ENQUIRY INTO THE CAUSES OF THE FREQUENT EXECUTIONS AT *TYBURN*:

AND

A PROPOSAL *for some* REGULATIONS *concerning* FELONS *in* PRISON, *and the good Effects to be Expected from them.*

To which is Added,
A Discourse on TRANSPORTATION, and a Method to render that Punishment more Effectual.

By *B. MANDEVILLE*, M. D.

Oderunt peccare Mali formidine Pœnæ.

LONDON,
Printed: And Sold by *J. Roberts* in *Warwick-Lane*.
MDCCXXV.

23. NICHOLAS SAUNDERSON (1682–1739)

Manuscript copy of his lectures on hydrostatics, pneumatics, optics and other topics in the physical sciences, c. 1734.

In the early eighteenth century the physical sciences at Cambridge were dominated by Newton's revolutionary ideas. Although Newton spent most of his later years in London, many of his disciples were in Cambridge and crowds flocked to their lectures to hear of the startling new discoveries. One of the most successful lecturers was Nicholas Saunderson, who held the Lucasian Chair of Mathematics from 1711 until his death in 1739. Saunderson, who was born in Yorkshire in 1682, was considered an excellent and effective teacher and a mathematician of the first order. The Brotherton Collection possesses a copy of his only published work, the *Elements of Algebra*, 1740.

Saunderson was remarkable in two respects. Firstly, he was largely self-taught. With the help of patrons he moved to Cambridge in 1707 and initially delivered private lectures. Secondly, Saunderson lost his sight at an early age, and yet was able to conceptualise and teach both mathematics and natural philosophy, including optics. No wonder Saunderson attracted considerable admiration and attention, and he was frequently discussed by philosophers and essayists throughout the eighteenth century.

The large number of extant copies of Saunderson's lectures on natural philosophy attests to their popularity and to the trade which existed in such manuscripts. This copy is one of the most attractive and was prepared with considerable care from another manuscript. It is not known who owned it or when it was written, but internal evidence suggests that it does not predate 1734, a date consistent with the watermark. An earlier manuscript of some of Saunderson's lectures, with others by his friend Gervase Holmes, is also in the Brotherton Collection.

Some other manuscript items and about 300 printed scientific books of the seventeenth and eighteenth centuries in the Brotherton Collection complement the more extensive collection of such works in the Brotherton Library. A comprehensive general survey by P. B. Wood and J. V. Golinski was published in The British Journal for the History of Science, *vol. 14, no. 48 (1981).*

We have large groups of first and early editions of works by Newton, including the 1687 Principia Mathematica *and* Opticks, *1704 (initialled 'S.M.', probably Samuel Molyneux the astronomer-politician), and by Robert Boyle, including Edmund Burke's copy of the* Works, *1774. Branches of science particularly well covered are optics and the calculus. Outstanding amongst a few foreign-printed works is Descartes's* Discours de la methode, *1637, a fine copy inscribed 'Liber Tho. Dennesun. 1646' in a contemporary binding.*

Besides the Saunderson lectures, we have the manuscript Opera Mathematica, c. *1700, of an unidentified Edward Thornycroft, perhaps related to the baronet Sir John Thornycroft, and mathematical notes of about the same date in the papers of John Salvio, tutor to the Ward family of Hooton Pagnell. There is also a series of letters written between 1765 and 1781 by J. T. Needham F.R.S. to his friend the French Ambassador at Turin; Needham, who spent much time in Europe and collaborated with Buffon, discusses contemporary intellectual affairs in the letters and mentions Voltaire, Rousseau and Wilkes.*

Hydrostatics.

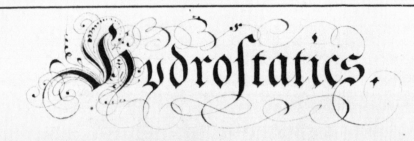

1. Hydrostatics, as first invented by Archimedes, consisted only in the Art of weighing Bodies in water, but as since improv'd comprehends the Nature and Properties of all Fluids whatsoever.

Of Fluidity in general.

2. A Fluid according to S.r Isaac Newtons definition is "Corpus "cujus partes vi cuicunq; illatæ cedunt et cedendo facillimè moventur "inter se". A Fluid differs from a liquid, humid, or moist, body in this, viz. Humidity is a mere relative property, depending upon a certain attractive force, between the Fluid and the parts of some particular bodies, which it is capable of wetting, that is of adhering to, and penetrating a little way into. Thus water is humid with respect to our hands, and quick-silver not: again, Quick-silver is humid with respect to most metals, and Water not with respect to the Feathers of Water-fowls, and the Leaves of most plants —— In S.r Isaac Newton's Def. it is requir'd that the parts of a Fluid not only yield to the slightest touch, as powders do, but they must also "cedendo facillimè moveri inter se, not only change place absolutely as powders when condens'd but also easily slide over one another, so that the whole be not press'd more on one part than on another, which does not happen by condensation.

3. But

24. LORD BYRON (1788–1824)

Autograph manuscript of an unfinished story in prose, 1816.

Near Geneva on 27 May 1816, Byron and Shelley met for the first time and immediately became friends, sharing their voluntary exile in rented houses near the lake on which they sailed together. In mid-June, the weather bad, their tireless conversation turned to the supernatural and at Byron's suggestion it was agreed that he, Shelley and his wife, and their companions Claire Clairmont and John Polidori would each write a ghost story. Shelley, finding the task uncongenial, did not fully participate, Polidori's ideas were derided though he later published *The Vampyre*, 1819, and Claire, uncertain of her relationship with Byron, could not find a theme. However, Mary Shelley's story, inspired by a nightmare she claimed, was to become the prodigious *Frankenstein* and Byron began the story the first page of the original manuscript of which is illustrated here.

Byron later sent the 15-page fragment to his publisher John Murray, stating in the covering letter (15 May 1819) 'I never went on with it — as you will perceive by the date. — I began it in an old account-book of Miss Milbanke's . . .'; the printed columns of the book may be seen. Byron suggested publication in *The Edinburgh Magazine*, simply to distinguish it from Polidori's work which was rumoured to be Byron's; Murray in fact published it with *Mazeppa*, 1819, much annoying Byron — 'be damned to you' he protested in a letter of 20 March 1820. The published version, besides the customary alteration of punctuation and spelling, changes one word of the manuscript and omits another: as Byron wrote to Murray on another occasion (24 September 1818) 'Consult the M.S. *always*'.

Most of our Byron manuscripts and letters were originally owned by his friend John Cam Hobhouse, whose own early transcription of four Byron poems includes 'Love and Death' headed 'the last he ever wrote'. Outstanding among the items wholly or partly in Byron's hand is Mary Shelley's fair copy of Mazeppa *made at Byron's request in 1818 and revised and corrected by him. The many early editions of Byron's printed works include, for example, ten genuine and spurious editions of* English Bards and Scotch Reviewers *published before 1818 and the exceptionally rare* Fare Thee Well, *1816.*

The early editons of Shelley's work present, besides material in the Novello-Cowden Clarke collection, include Zastrozzi, *1810,* Queen Mab, *1813, together with the later Clark and Carlile editions, Leigh Hunt's copy of* The Cenci, *1819, with various passages marked by him, and* Epipsychidion, *1821, one of 100 copies printed. The only Shelley autograph is a letter to Ollier, 22 February 1817; a couple of letters from Godwin to Shelley's solicitor concern their financial affairs in mid-1817.*

With discernment unusual amongst contemporary writers, Byron declared 'Crabbe's the man'. The Collection has over 80 Crabbe letters, most of them in groups formed by A. M. Broadley, who largely based The Romance of an Elderly Poet, *1913, on a sequence of 46 to Elizabeth Charter. Other autograph Crabbe items are four notebooks including some verse, part of a manuscript of* The Parish Register *and three drafts of sermons. We also have manuscripts of, and many letters to and from, another Suffolk poet, Bernard Barton.*

June 17th 1816.

In the year 17— having for some time determined
on a journey through countries not hitherto much
frequented by travellers I set out accompanied by
a friend whom I shall designate by the name of
Augustus Darvell. — — He was a few years my elder — and a
man of considerable fortune — and antient family —
advantages which an extensive capacity prevented
him alike from undervaluing or overrating. —
Some peculiar circumstances in his private history
had rendered him to me an object of attention
of interest and even of regard, which neither the
reserve of his manners — nor occasional indications
of an inquietude at times nearly approaching to aliena=
=tion of mind — could extinguish. — —
I was yet young in life which I had begun early
but my intimacy with him was of a recent date
we had been educated at the same schools & university.

25. SIR WALTER SCOTT (1771–1832)

Autograph leaf from the manuscript of The Siege of Malta, *1832.*

Towards the end of his life Sir Walter Scott's health was severely affected by a series of strokes. In late 1831 he set out for Malta on a frigate of the Royal Navy in the hope that a journey to a warmer climate might prove restorative and with the idea of using the visit to the island as the occasion for a novel based on the 1565 siege of the Knights of St John by the Turks. He envisaged this work as the culmination of the Waverley series, one that would bring the annotated collected edition of his novels (on which he had been working since 1828) to the good round number fifty volumes. But his ill-health told too heavily against him: the manuscript he produced turned out to be a disappointingly incoherent document, lacking continuity and logical consistency overall, and often unintelligible or nonsensical word by word and sentence by sentence. So radical are its defects that *The siege* has defied all attempts to extract from it a publishable novel.

The greatest part of the 150-page manuscript is now in the Berg Collection of the New York Public Library. While the manuscript was still at Abbotsford it seems to have been the occasional practice of the Scott family to give a single leaf or, more usually, a fragment of a leaf, to especially favoured friends or admirers of Scott. The Brotherton leaf — like another such leaf in the Beinecke Library of Yale University — presumably became separated from the manuscript in this way.

Lord Brotherton had great admiration for Scott and collected many of his autograph letters; most were published for him in Some Unpublished Letters of Sir Walter Scott, *1932, which sadly Brotherton did not live to see in print. Amongst the Scott correspondents are Southey, Crabbe, Maria Edgeworth, and the critics J. W. Croker and John Wilson; a letter to John Richardson includes Scott's draft of his own family pedigree. Central to our large collection of Scott's printed works is a complete set of first editions of the Waverley novels, 1814–32; all are as issued in their original boards, as is our copy of Scott's first published work, his version of Bürger,* The Chase, and William and Helen, *1796.*

We also have many letters by Scott's friends and associates. A portion of the correspondence of Scott's great publisher Archibald Constable includes long series of letters from William Blackwood, Brougham, Amelia Opie, the Duke of Roxburghe, Anna Seward, and Sydney Smith. There are also many letters to his and Scott's friend John Richardson from Thomas Campbell, the poet and, at one time, would-be collaborator with Scott on the 'British Poets' project. Perhaps the most revealing correspondence is between Alexander Blair and John Wilson ('Christopher North'), the mercurial mainstay, with Scott's biographer Lockhart, of Blackwood's Magazine; *the many Wilson and Blair letters, 1809–52, show Wilson's enormous debt to his lifelong friend's judgement and advice. There are also letters to Wilson from others.*

joined itself to high birth great reputation and long practice in arms which made death however painful preferable an honoured name to the least slur on reputation. The effect of what might still be called their chivalrous courage extended itself amon the more ordinary soldiers who felt the honour of sharing and in their ranks and mounting to danger under their guidance and resolutely adopting the same alternative of a successful resistance or an honourable Death crowned with the praises of all Europe and the blessing of the holy power whom it worshiped through all its kingdoms.

The very classes into which the defenders of Malta were divided tended also to animate the enthusiasm of defence with which the whole were animated. The Pacha or Turkish commander felt a great difficulty in ascending to the cavalier of the fortification out of the trench by which the besiegers made their approach to it for the defence of the besieged was so obstinate that for a time he despaired of forcing his way. The very women of the garrison assisted in manning the cavalier and casting down heavy stones artificial fireworks of different kinds and supplying their own friends with food medicine and assistance to leave the works when so wounded as to be unable to continue their defence of them any longer. They were encouraged to continue a species of resistance which seemed scarce natural to their sex by the enthusiasm of the moment and especially by the pains which had been taken to raise the cavalier to a height which could not be easily commanded by the fort of attack so that for a long time the shot of the besiegers was not greatly injurious to those of either sex who maintained their defence of the Cavalier of Saint Elmo.

But on the cessation of the first days combat Piali immediately he had devised a stratagem by which he should attain the desired superiority by which the assailants might either attain the desired superiority over the defence from which hitherto so failed a force. He therefore employed a strong body of skillful artizans who had not been employed in the trenches on the days which had just closed & distributing the task among as could be well employed at the same time he employed them in constructing a certain carriage for a cannon of so great size that it might be best compared to a double tower the inner division of which could be raised out of that which was outward by means of screws and consequently he established its station where the Turkish battery approach most near to the Cavalier of the Knights by the fire from which the approaches &c

26. SAMUEL TAYLOR COLERIDGE (1772–1834)

Autograph essay on the emancipation of slaves, 1833.

All his life Coleridge had an intense and informed interest in politics, particularly when they had to do with social justice. Among his most impassioned concerns was the abolition of slavery. One of his finest essays in *The Watchman* (25 March 1796), 'On the Slave Trade', advocated a public boycott of sugar and rum as a means of exerting pressure for abolition — '[the fine lady] sips a beverage sweetened with human blood', he wrote. After the British slave trade was abolished in 1807, the struggle to free existing slaves in the West Indies continued to a climax in the Abolition Act of 1833.

This unpublished note, of which the third page is illustrated here, was sent by Coleridge for comment to his friend Thomas Pringle (1789–1834), a poet and Secretary of the Anti-Slavery Society. Clearly it was written during the debate immediately before the August 1833 legislation. The emancipation scheme proposed by Edward Stanley for the Government included a system of 'apprenticeship', whereby, for 12 years, the slave would receive a form of training for freedom, and some payment out of which he would eventually buy that freedom. Concerned here with the training rather than the manifestly unjust financial aspect of 'Mr Stanley's 12 years apprenticeship', Coleridge suggests that freedom should be earned more rapidly and usefully through specific educational achievements. Earlier in the note, he deplores the sectarian rivalry of missionaries and others as a poor example of Christian citizenship for slaves.

Pringle knew Coleridge's views on the financial aspect independently, for his separate unpublished letter furiously attacking those seeking compensation for losing slaves is also in the Brotherton Collection. All society may share the guilt of having permitted slavery, he admits, but those who have chosen to profit from owning slaves should not expect others to share the costs of abolition.

The writers of other unpublished letters to Pringle in the Brotherton Collection, 1828 to 1834, presented by Dr T. E. Harvey, include Clare ('like a church mouse I live as I can & take little profit of the sermon'), Darley, Galt, Hogg, Lytton, Lord Macaulay, Miss Mitford, Rogers, Scott, and the young Tennyson, as well as the Abolitionists Buxton, Clarkson, Zachary Macaulay, and Wilberforce.

Amongst our several first editions of Coleridge's works is a Zapolya, *1817, said to have been Wordsworth's; we also have the London issue of the first edition of* Lyrical Ballads, *1798, and a second edition, 1800, with both issues of the second volume which was first printed then. Besides other Wordsworth first editions, we have a letter in his wife's hand signed by him, 1835, and correspondence received by William Hale White ('Mark Rutherford') when writing his* Description of . . . Wordsworth & Coleridge Manuscripts, *1897. There are Wordsworth and Coleridge references in our numerous letters of Robert Southey, mostly addressed to his friend John May; we also have some leaves of Southey's commonplace notes and the autograph draft of his angry 'letter' to Henry Brougham, 1818, most of which he was dissuaded by friends from publishing. De Quincey is represented by an autograph note of 1837 on his health and diet.*

the process, even for their own safety and benefit — would be sufficient to
make it possible to divide the Slaves of each Plantation into
5 or 6 classes — according to their existing acquirements — all being
made to know that they were to be successively made free — Some
little medal or other mark of distinction might announce the
fully free Servant — and perhaps another badge for the immediate
Expectants, the Candidates of the First Class — every step of
promotion being the ~~premium of their progress in the~~ reading,
and writing, and the fundamental truths of Religion and
Morality, conjoined with their orderly conduct. Thus every
year, yea, every half-year, would increase the number
of those who felt an interest and a distinction in
the system — while the near prospect of possessing
the same would render the remainder more docile —
more open to the conviction, first, that it was in their own
power to expedite their emancipation, & secondly, that it was
withheld from them, not arbitrarily, but for their own welfare,
and in order to make it a real blessing — in order to
on the contrary, that their Master wishes this and the speedy accomplishment of this even
render them actually and not only nominally free. — x better
more than themselves.
a Zealous & able Body of Instructors, and with the concurrence
of the Masters, four fifths of the Slaves might be free in
the same number of years — and the remainder, of course,
the least hopeful subjects, might be without danger or offence
employed under police regulations on public works &c — I cannot
but prefer the chances of such a scheme, both for time and for the final
security of the Blacks to Mr Stanley's 12 years Apprenticeship — S. T. Coleridge

27. PATRICK BRANWELL BRONTË (1817–48)

The life of Feild Marshal the Right Honourable Alexan[d]er Percy, *autograph manuscript, 1835.*

In pursuit of Brontë manuscripts, Clement Shorter, man of letters and literary opportunist, tracked down Charlotte Brontë's widower, A. B. Nicholls, in 1895, exactly 40 years after her death. Shorter records that 'Mr Nicholls placed all the papers in his possession in my hands'. In fact, Nicholls discovered Brontë papers over a period of weeks, stored about his house in a small Irish town; one batch sent to Shorter, he wrote, 'I found in the bottom of a cupboard tied up in newspaper, where they had lain for nearly 30 years, and where had it not been for your visit, they must have remained during my lifetime, and most likely afterwards have been destroyed'.

Shorter may have saved the Brontë papers from oblivion, but the story following the rescue is sad. Most were sold to T. J. Wise, Nicholls receiving the false impression, as letters in the Brotherton Collection show, that they were destined for a London museum. Instead, Wise kept some of the manuscripts and sold the rest privately in a manner which has confounded scholars ever since; the microscopic writings of the Brontës as children were often split up page by page and widely scattered.

The whereabouts of this manuscript by the young Branwell, Charlotte's brother, and another sold with it, *Real Life in Verdopolis*, were unknown to Brontë scholars from 1904 until 1980 when they were bought by the Brotherton Collection. Of Branwell's manuscripts Nicholls wrote to Shorter 'There are a large number . . . but I don't suppose you care to have them'; Shorter and Wise certainly did, as does the Brotherton Collection for different reasons.

Lord Brotherton's collection of manuscripts by members of the Brontë family was strongest in those of the ill-fated Branwell. They include his Letters from an Englishman *in six miniature volumes,* Caractacus. A Dramatic Poem, *his translation of Horace's* Odes, *numerous Angrian prose fragments and his extraordinary illustrated letters to J. B. Leyland.*

The Brontës' father is represented by scarce printed works, their mother by a letter to her fiancé beginning 'My dear saucy Pat', 18 November 1812, and her autograph essay The Advantages of Poverty in Religious Concerns. *A manuscript dialogue attributed to Anne Brontë is in the same notebook as transcriptions of many of Charlotte's poems made by her husband. We have several good letters by Charlotte and two of her manuscript French* devoirs. *Rarest of the many printed Brontë works present is the Aylott and Jones issue of the sisters' poems, 1846.*

References to Charlotte Brontë appear in our autograph letters, about 90 in number, of her biographer, the novelist Mrs Gaskell; we have transcriptions of many more, with copious notes by C. K. Shorter and a manuscript review of Mary Barton *by Emily Winkworth. Of W. M. Thackeray, the author whom Charlotte Brontë most admired, we have some 20 letters, two manuscript ballads, a page of* Philip *and an original illustration modified for* Vanity Fair. *Much of this was collected by Dr Eric Millar, as were some 170 of our Dickens letters; these include letters to G. H. Lewes, and we have more letters to him, his family and to George Eliot, from Trollope, Charlotte Brontë again, and others.*

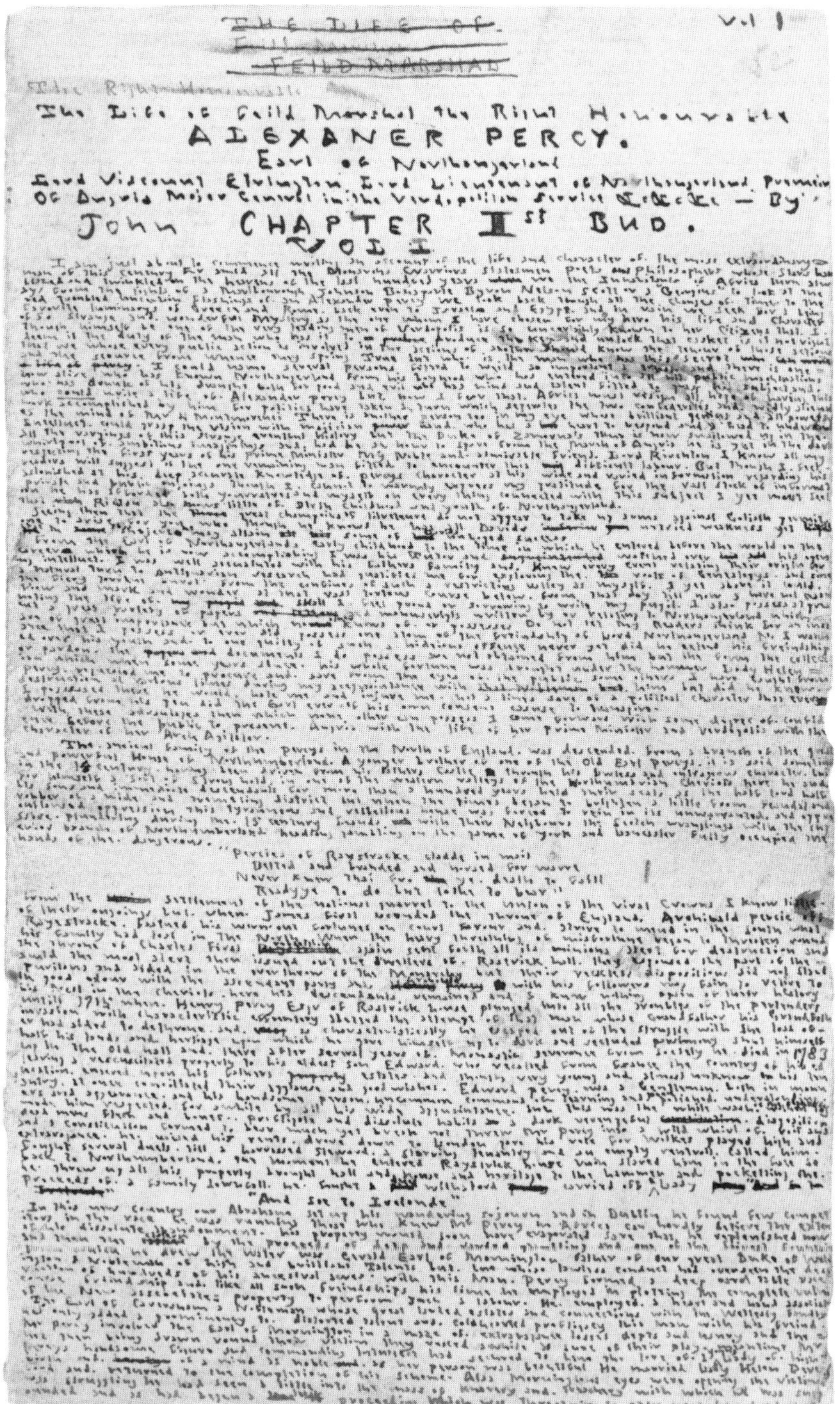
Vol 1
The Life of Feild Marshal the Right Honourable
ALEXANER PERCY.
Earl of Northangerland
CHAPTER Ist
VOL I

28. MATTHEW ARNOLD (1822–88)

Autograph autobiographical note in a notebook compiled by his mother, 1836.

At the age of 13 in 1836, a very bright, cool and witty Matthew Arnold who was anxious to impress his mother was invited, by her, to write a short autobiography. By then Matthew's father Dr Thomas Arnold was gaining fame as Rugby School's reforming headmaster. First, Matthew's elder sister Jane, at 14, wrote a brief account of her own life for a small, leather-bound notebook in which Mrs Arnold was recording poems written by her children. Then, since Jane had begun *her* autobiography modestly with 'I was born on August 1st 1821. I am told but cannot remember it, that when I was a baby I was very ill', Matthew Arnold aimed to show off his wit. He begins his sprightly autobiography by mocking history-books: 'Tradition says that I was born at Laleham in 1822 on the 24th of December'. Then he boasts about his memory, claims he keeps no vulgar 'string of facts' in his head but 'only abstruse ones', and wryly remembers having asked one of Papa's pupils for a *bough* and getting a *bow*. But he recalls his own 'crooked legs, & wearing irons', since when he had rickets he had hobbled about in heavy orthopaedic leg-irons and screamed and misbehaved in early childhood at Laleham — when, he says, he was 'obstinate'.

The odd pathos of the 'pig killed' and of his other memories foreshadows his career as the elegiac poet who wrote 'The scholar gipsy' and 'Thyrsis'. His insouciance, glee and intelligence at 13 remind one, too, of his future career as a School Inspector and of the discernment of his *Essays in Criticism* and *Culture and Anarchy* to come.

We are chiefly indebted for our collection of Arnold family papers to Mrs Mary Moorman, the distinguished Wordsworth scholar and descendant of Dr Thomas Arnold and his wife. Six of Dr Arnold's journal-notebooks here range over many years and deal with his travels, his classical studies and Rugby School affairs, while another six compiled by Mrs Mary Arnold, including that illustrated, chronicle family events; there are over 250 of their autograph letters, several further manuscripts and many letters by their children. We have other items by the young Matthew Arnold and, from later in his life, a series of his letters to Robert Browning. One of the family notebooks includes an autograph poem by Clough and notes by A. P. Stanley.

Three other sets of autograph correspondence may be mentioned here. Of J. S. Mill, who greatly admired Dr Arnold as a classical historian, we have much-revised drafts of some 70 letters to John Sterling, Bain, Mazzini, Villari, and others. John Ruskin's approach to classical literature less impressed Matthew Arnold as Oxford Professor of Poetry, to which post Ruskin declined to succeed him; Ruskin is seen more privately in our unpublished series of his letters to his Winnington schoolgirl friends. As Professor, Arnold also declared that Ichabod Charles Wright's translation of the Iliad *had 'no proper reason for existing', though he later made a memorable apology; we have Wright's very large correspondence on his* Iliad, *and also his Dante, with Brougham, Gladstone, Kingsley, Panizzi, and many others.*

and Worcester. And another holliday, the same party with the additions of Mary and Miss Rutland went into Scotland as far as Inverary. In the December 1831 we first went to the Lakes, to Rydal. The summer after that to Braythey. Then to Fox-ghyll. Then to Allan Bank. Then the rest went again to Allan Bank but I stayed at Laleham. Then Papa built a house called Fox How. and now we go there every hollidays. –

Tradition says that I was born at Laleham in 1822 on the 24th of December. I think my memory must be very good, for I remember such quantities of things wch occurred there. I have not however any string of facts in my head, but only abstruse ones. One of the first things I

18

remember is my asking one of Papa's pupils who were very kind to us, one morning after breakfast to get me a bough, and he greatly obliged me by making a bow. We used also to be in the parlour after breakfast, putting together our dissected maps. I also remember when one of the pupils gave a book of beasts to Papa, and the going out to see a particular pig killed, & seeing a great hole dug till they came to water, & being carried about the garden by Spot, and being obstinate, and going up to London about my crooked legs, & wearing irons, & seeing Aunt Lydia copy the house from the Lawn. Also cutting the thistles with Willy Buckland & Jane & Tom, in the garden.

29. ALGERNON CHARLES SWINBURNE (1837–1909)

Autograph manuscript copy of 'Thalassius', 1879, with annotations by the printer of the poem.

'Thalassius', meaning 'of the sea' or 'sea-born', was described by Swinburne himself in a letter to Edmund Gosse dated 10 October 1879 as 'a symbolical quasi-autobiographical poem after the fashion of Shelley or of Hugo, concerning the generation, birth and rearing of a by-blow of Amphitrite's . . . reared like Ion in the temple service of Apollo. It would be a pretty subject', Swinburne continued, 'but when should I hear the last of my implied arrogance and self-conceit?'. Despite the light-hearted and off-hand tone of his remarks, Swinburne must in fact have already started, or have been on the very brink of starting, composition of 'Thalassius'. Opposite line 162 of the manuscript here illustrated is the date in Swinburne's hand 'Monday Oct. 27 / 79'. What is more, his purpose was extremely serious. It was nothing less than the spiritual autobiography of a poet.

The Brotherton Collection is fortunate in possessing a splendid manuscript of this most important poem. It is an autograph fair copy, with revisions, written on one side only of 21 folio leaves of blue laid paper, and on both sides of another. The watermarks are 'SAWSTON / 1878' and 'VALLEYFIELD'. The title 'Thalassius' is in Swinburne's hand, but the note at the head of the first page 'lines to be numbered as marked' is not, and nor is the pencil numeration of the lines. This is because the manuscript was used as copy for the printer, and was marked up as such. Being the printer's copy, however, does mean that this manuscript is the latest text over which we know the poet had sole control. This makes it of great importance, though in fact it only differs from the published text in three places.

The Brotherton Collection has an array of Swinburne manuscripts and letters far too large to be described here in detail; most derive from the collections of Swinburne's friend Sir Edmund Gosse and T. J. Wise, who together edited the Bonchurch edition of his works. We also have much correspondence of Swinburne's devoted guardian Theodore Watts-Dunton, some with the poet's family. All this has close links with our hundreds of letters of Christina, W.M., and especially D. G. Rossetti, Burne-Jones, F. M. Brown, and others, again largely first accumulated by the tireless Wise; from other sources we have letters of related figures like Holman Hunt.

Of Swinburne's hero Landor we have various autograph fragments, including an imaginary conversation between Virgil and Horace. From his early teens Swinburne preferred Landor's work to Tennyson's, though the Laureate generously praised him. The most important of our several Tennyson items is from his teens, a copy of Poems, by two brothers, *1827, in which Alfred has identified by hand his own poems and those by his brothers Charles and Frederick. Tennyson was parodied in Swinburne's* Heptalogia *along with Robert Browning, of whom we have some letters as well as ten illustrated manuscript stories by Browning's father. Swinburne idolised Victor Hugo, seen here intimately as recipient of nearly 500 letters from his mistress Juliette Drouet. We also have correspondence of two other French writers, Vigny and Dumas* fils, *and autograph manuscripts of a dozen novels in English by the Dutch-born 'Maarten Maartens', who treasured his meeting with the aged Swinburne.*

As lighten something even of all man's doom
Even from the labouring womb
Even to the seal set on the unopening tomb! 100 Hy
(Monday Oct. 27/79)
And there the loving light of song & love
Shall wrap & lap round & impend above,
Imperishable: & all springs born ~~perfume~~ illume
Their ~~names~~ sleep with ~~sweeter~~ high ~~sound~~ thoughts than ~~song of~~ wake the love
~~And all that's blowing bloom. sweeter mix the heather sweet with broom~~
To mine, when the hill-side winds resume
The ~~a~~ marriage-song of heather-flower & broom
And all the joy thereof.

And hate the ~~high~~ song too taught him: hate of all
That brings or holds in thrall
Of spirit or flesh, free-born ere God began, 10
The holy body & sacred soul of man.
And wheresoever a curse was or a chain,
A throne for torment or a crown for bane
Rose, moulded out of poor men's molten pain,
There, said he, shd man's heaviest hate be set
Inexorably, to faint not or forget
Till the last warmth bled forth of the last vein
In flesh that none shd call a king's again,

30. VINCENT NOVELLO (1781–1861)

Autograph manuscript travel journal, 1829, with a lock of Mozart's hair.

Vincent Novello idolised Mozart, to him 'the Shakespeare of music'. In 1829, when he was contemplating writing the composer's biography, Novello heard that Mozart's sister, his fellow child-prodigy of the 1760s, lay blind and in distress in Salzburg. Promptly Novello organised a subscription of money for her from London musicians and he and his wife set off to present the gift in person. This act of generosity and homage to the memory of Mozart, who had died some 40 years earlier, allowed Novello to gather material for the biography, to observe the European musical scene and, incidentally, to arrange the musical education in Paris of his daughter Clara, who was to become a leading soprano of her time.

For much of their journey both Novellos kept journals, hurriedly written in fading pencil; they were published in 1955 as *A Mozart Pilgrimage*, edited by Rosemary Hughes, and are now in the Brotherton Collection. Vincent's was designed as a business-like set of notes, Mary Novello's more for her family to read, but the two complement and corroborate each other. They are full of observations of people and places, of art, architecture and music, particularly in churches, but most interesting are the notes on Mozart gathered from his family.

When the Novellos asked Mozart's widow for a piece of his hair as a memento, she at first claimed to have none but, relenting later as trust grew, she gave them the lock shown here with Vincent's blurred journal note recording the event. The hair is a rich, soft, chestnut-brown, contrasting evocatively with the coarser, grey, uncurled lock of Beethoven's also here, given to the Novellos on another occasion by J. A. Stumpff, Beethoven's harp-maker acquaintance.

The Novello-Cowden Clarke collection was presented to the Brotherton Collection in 1953 by Donna Nerina Medici di Marignano Gigliucci and Contessa Bona Gigliucci. It has two main parts, the papers and correspondence of the Novello family and a library of books collected by the Cowden Clarkes. The two sections are intimately connected, for Mary Victoria, the wife of Keats's friend Charles Cowden Clarke, was the eldest of Vincent Novello's eleven children.

Vincent Novello himself, London-born of Italian parents, was an organist, composer, and founder of the music-publishing business which still bears his name. The diary illustrated is one of various documents concerning him in the collection, including some of his music in manuscript. We also have many papers of his eldest son Joseph Alfred, his dynamic partner in the publishing venture and a restless inventor and investor. Other Novello children were also highly talented. There is much here about the brilliant singing career of Clara, whose grand-daughters gave us the collection; the autograph manuscript of her Reminiscences *differs somewhat from the published version of 1910. Many drawings and paintings attest to the 'genuine talent', as William Etty described it, of Edward, who died sadly young. Another daughter Cecilia retired from a promising stage career to marry the dramatist T. J. Serle.*

in the fulfilment of his enviable task
wh. will be equally honorable to
himself – to his immortal father – & to his
native Country – of which that father is
the most brilliant ornament.

He wrote a most charming little Trio
of his own composition beginning

in my album & I had the pleasure of giving
his acceptance of one of my water colour sketches
to wear for my sake [illegible] – little [illegible]
of these very high gratification [illegible]
derived from having so [illegible]
formed his acquaintance

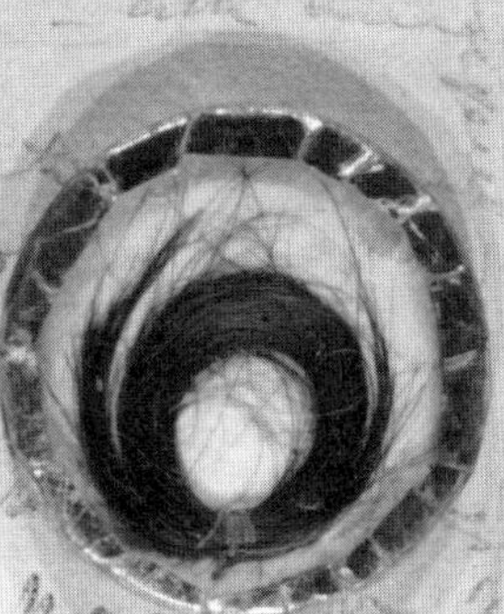

The widow who had [illegible]
small quantity left of Mozart's [illegible]
hair – was so kind as to share that treasured [illegible] with
me (which I esteem as a very high & flattering
compliment) – she consents to accept
– in return a little gold Brooch, which I ha[illegible]

[illegible]

31. CHARLES DICKENS (1812–70)

Autograph letter to Mary Cowden Clarke and Emma Novello, 19 September 1848.

Mrs Clarke and Dickens had been introduced to each other by Leigh Hunt at an evening party in April 1848 when Mrs Clarke, fresh from an amateur appearance as Mrs Malaprop, offered to play Dame Quickly in the amateur theatricals being organised by Dickens to raise funds to endow a curatorship at Shakespeare's birthplace. Mrs Clarke spent the summer months acting, under the direction of Dickens, in various plays and farces in London and provincial centres. She was accompanied by her young sister Emma Novello.

In *Recollections of Writers* (1878) Mrs Clarke wrote that she cherished the memory of Dickens 'still with as fond an idolatry as she felt during that joyous period of her life when in privileged holiday companionship with him'. She recalled 'My sister Emma having helped me with the designs for a blotting-case I embroidered for Charles Dickens, he sent us the accompanying sprightly letter of acknowledgment, signing it with various names of parts he had played, written in the most respectively characteristic handwritings. These names in gold letters upon green morocco leather, formed the corners to the green watered silk covering in which I had the blotting-book bound; the centres having on one side a wreath of heartsease and forget-me-nots surrounding the initials "Y.G."; on the other a group of roses and rose-buds, worked in floss silks of natural colours'. Y.G., or Young Gas, was the name Dickens had given himself as manager of the theatrical company.

The Novellos' convivial London household attracted many literary visitors. Leigh Hunt was a very close friend and through him Charles Cowden Clarke joined the family circle, marrying Vincent's daughter Mary Victoria. In earlier years the Lambs were also friends, Keats and Shelley less intimate family acquaintances. All these contacts are recorded in material in the Collection.

There are over 130 letters from Leigh Hunt and many copies of his books with autograph annotation; there are letters also from the Lambs and a farce copied from Charles Lamb's manuscript 'without permission'. Vincent Novello's copy of Shelley's Prometheus Unbound *is inscribed 'The Gift of the Author. Sepr. 15. 1820' and Shelley's* Posthumous Poems, *1824, bound with his* Adonais, *Pisa, 1821, has three further poems by him written in by Mary Shelley. Besides a revealing reference to 'Junkets' in a Hunt letter, Keats is remembered in Charles Cowden Clarke's copy of Monckton Milnes's* Life, *1848, with annotations in which the owner, from personal knowledge, contradicts some statements in the work.*

From the 1830s onwards the collection increasingly reflects Cowden Clarke friendships. They corresponded with Mrs Gaskell and with Douglas Jerrold, a great favourite of Mary, whose own literary labours are represented. Letters like that illustrated mark the intimate friendship with Dickens and presentation copies of his works are outstanding in the 1,000 volumes, recreational rather than scholarly, of the Cowden Clarke's books here. A descriptive booklet about the Novello-Cowden Clarke collection is available.

out of our minds. at least we hope so, for such remembrances can only go out with our five senses, and we hope to keep ours, for these many years.

Dear friends

Yours ever

Shallow

Custalorum

Abraham Slender

Robert Flexible

Charles Coldstream [?]

Doctor Blank

Young Bass [?]

Bobadil

P. Snobbington.

Charles Dickens

(The Wicked [?] Manager.)

32. SIR EDMUND GOSSE (1849–1928)

Zoological Sketches Consisting of Description and Engravings of Animals, *autograph manuscript, 1858.*

These *Zoological Sketches* by E. W. Gosse 'M.A.' were produced by Edmund Gosse in 1858. He was nine in the September of that year. He was not an infant prodigy. His sketches, as he admits in *Father and Son*, were for the most part 'ludicrous pastiches' of the work his father, the marine biologist, P. H. Gosse, was engaged in at that time, *Actinologia Britannica*. This particular illustration may well be considered a portrait of the father himself. What he could not bear about the son's touching tribute (dedicated to 'Philip Henry Gosse with the Author's very best Love') was its lack of originality. Not only did the boy seem to show no artistic skill, his descriptions were often copied from other books, in the familiar manner of a child of that age nowadays, engaged on a school 'project'.

But Edmund's industry was entirely self-directed. As he wrote: 'My labours failed to make me a zoologist. . . Yet I cannot look upon the mental discipline as useless. It taught me to concentrate my attention . . . Moreover, it gave me the habit of going on with any piece of work I had in hand, not flagging because the interest or picturesqueness of the theme had declined, but pushing forth towards a definite goal'.

The father could not wholly condemn the curious obsession, though it seems to have been those endless hours Edmund spent poring over his 'books' in a stuffy box-room that first made his father realise he needed friends.

The M.A. the child added to his name is poignant when we realise that, when the time came, there was no chance for him to go to university. It was not until 1885, when he was Clark Lecturer at Cambridge, that Gosse was finally entitled to use the letters to which he had laid claim 27 years before.

The papers of Sir Edmund Gosse were acquired from his family by Lord Brotherton shortly after Gosse's death. They include some of his own manuscripts, from the products of his unusual childhood to mature critical and other works, and there are also manuscripts of his father P. H. Gosse. Most of Gosse's separately published printed works are present, several more scarce than Father and Son, *for which he is most widely remembered, and there are numerous photographs, drawings, miscellaneous documents, and memorabilia.*

The greater part of the papers consists of letters received by Gosse over a period of 60 years, throughout which, even in the earliest days after his arrival in London in 1867, he was in personal contact with many outstanding literary and artistic contemporaries. He was befriended by Swinburne and encouraged as a poet by Tennyson, Browning, and D. G. Rossetti. Later he was a colleague of Austin Dobson, the English champion of Ibsen and latterly Gide, Henry James's confidant and a close friend of Thomas Hardy into their very old age, when they talked 'like two antediluvian animals sporting in the primeval slime', as Gosse put it. There are hundreds of letters from these writers amongst the thousands to Gosse in the Collection.

The Man.

It is to many hart to belive that a Man is an animal, however, he is the type of the class Bimana, or 2-handed animals.
As the Man is so very well known many partitulars are unnesersary, exept to mention the varietes of

33. VISCOUNT HALDANE (1856–1928)

Autograph letter to Edmund Gosse, 12 September 1917.

R. B. Haldane, Secretary of State for War from 1905 to 1912, had been the target of sustained abuse in the press on account of his supposed sympathies for Germany; and when he received 2,600 hostile letters on a single day, he entrusted their disposal to his kitchen maid. As first Viscount Haldane of Cloan, he was Lord Chancellor from 1912 until forced from office by Unionist hostility in 1915. Haldane behaved with stoic dignity but felt acutely the refusal of the Foreign Office and the Prime Minister to publish the record of his dealings with Germany, and especially of his talks in Berlin of February 1912 with the Emperor William II and leading German statesmen.

Having compiled an account of his actions, Haldane showed it to Harold Begbie, who published a book defending his record, and C. P. Scott, Editor of the *Manchester Guardian*, which printed several articles in the first days of September 1917, to the natural satisfaction of Haldane himself and with the approval of Sir Edward Grey, who had been ejected from the Foreign Office in December 1916. Throughout his difficulties, Haldane found a refreshing and sympathetic friend in Edmund Gosse, who as Librarian of the House of Lords from 1904 to 1914 had observed the problems of government at first hand but independently of any faction. Haldane once told him 'You are the most perfect of friends and you have been a tower of strength to me in these troubled times'.

This letter recounts private conversations between Haldane and Grey. Grey said with emotion 'I was overpraised, and then deposed. You were attacked bitterly. And yet all I did to save Europe was not comparable to what the nation and the world owes to your military re-organisation. It saved Paris and it has saved the war'. That judgement the historian might wish to dispute, at least in part; but as Haldane characteristically remarked, 'This was at least handsome'. When they discussed what more could have been done before the war, had they known then all that would follow, Grey commented 'Nothing more'. Another point in the letter deserves record. Grey believed that the war would be won somehow by the autumn of 1918; the Russian Revolution might delay but could not avert this consummation.

The variety of Gosse's correspondence provides clear evidence of his exceptional capacity for making friends. After becoming Librarian of the House of Lords, the scope of his contacts increased, particularly amongst politicians who valued his advice on literary matters and sparkling conversation. Haldane was much the closest of Gosse's political friends, but many others are represented in the letters, such as Asquith, Balfour, and Curzon. Though gratified by the regard of the eminent, Gosse was also a generous friend to aspiring writers: Siegfried Sassoon especially was helped, and at Yeats's request, even Joyce, whose work Gosse loathed.

A catalogue of the Gosse correspondence, albeit rather incomplete, was published in 1950 and remains available. It was introduced by Gosse's son Dr Philip Gosse, who with other family members has added many gifts, including Sargent's fine portrait of Sir Edmund in 1885 and others, in bronze, by Hamo Thornycroft.

papers have, without recanting,
but still faithfully, reproduced
the substance of the narrative.

Edward Grey has been
here for two days & has just
left. It was a very pleasant
visit. We talked frankly.
He had read the M. Guardian
view & endorses it & approves
of Scott's action. He said, with
some emotion, 'I (Grey) was over-
-praised, & then deposed. You
(H) were attacked bitterly. And
yet all I (G.) did to save
Europe was not comparable
to what the nation & the world
owes to your military reorgani-
-sation. It saved Paris & it

has saved the war.' This was
at least handsome. He
& I went over policy in the past.
I asked him what else, had
he known all that would come,
we could have done. He said
there was nothing more. Had
we tried to alarm the world
in 1906, assuming that we
had found ground for doing
so, he holds that Germany would
have attacked before we
were any of us ready. We
could not, again, have attempted
to raise a Continental army
on a large scale — even under
peaceful conditions, for a similar

34. RAYMOND LISTER (born 1919)

The Unicorn of the Marshes, *miniature painting, 1947.*

The painter writes:

Philip Gosse and his wife Anna Gordon Keown the novelist were a delightful couple, opposite in many ways, yet a perfect ensemble. Philip was very much a man of this world who gave a wholly misleading impression of cynicism, which hid a romantic *tendresse.* Anna's heart was bared, she was full of Irish whimsy and she possessed a Blake-like innocence, that allowed her to derive intense pleasure from the sight of a single daffodil in bloom, or of a few nasturtiums arranged on a dish of cobalt blue. Above all she loved animals, dogs and cats especially, and I have many memories of her seated in her chair, cuddling Philip's tabby-cat Ninny, as demanding a character as Hardy's dog, Wessex.

Not only real animals, but Anna also understood mythological beasts and knew that, just as successive generations have invented and added to the personages of King Arthur, King Lear and Robin Hood, to provide vicarious fulfilment of people's aspirations and beliefs, so certain fabulous animals, among them the yale, the wyvern and the unicorn, beginning perhaps in heraldry, embraced similar functions. This is especially true of the unicorn with his particular association with virginity — so well expressed in the tapestries of 'La dame au licorne' in La Musée de Cluny in Paris. So, when I painted my miniature 'The Unicorn of the Marshes', it was natural that I should give it to Anna.

Anna Gordon Keown died in 1957. During the following year, in his late wife's memory, Dr Philip Gosse presented a number of books, manuscripts and letters associated with her and their friends to the Brotherton Collection. Seeing this as a beginning, not an end in itself, Dr Gosse also provided an endowment to allow further material, particularly by modern English poets, to be added.

Besides copies of all Miss Keown's works, the founding gift includes a delightful group of some 200 books formerly owned by the Gosses, with presentation volumes from friends such as Clifford Bax, John Carter, Siegfried Sassoon (who wrote the preface to Miss Keown's Collected Poems, *1953), and J. C. Squire; some books from Sir Edmund Gosse's library, including a presentation copy from Patmore of his* The Angel in the House*; diverting items retrieved from Cambridge bookstalls, like* Diary of an Ennuyée, *1826, and* New Songs of the Cambridge Lotos Club, *1881; and Lord Alfred Douglas's scarce and scandalous* The Rossiad, *1916. Amongst the manuscripts the Gosses' own are most plentiful, but several of their friends are represented, Frances Cornford for example. Family friends are still more evident in the correspondence preserved; Sassoon, Sir Geoffrey Keynes, A. J. A. Symons, the Sitwells, and others appear, with some long sequences of letters. And there are more items by Mr Lister, including several original miniatures illustrating his* Virgil's Second Eclogue, *1958. Manuscripts added later include work by Blunden and Dom Moraes and many works published in limited editions are amongst the printed books purchased for the Anna Gordon Keown collection.*

35. THOMAS HARDY (1840–1928)

Autograph letter, with additions by Florence Hardy, to Edward Clodd, 11 February 1915.

Hardy met Clodd, who was just one month younger than himself, in or around the year 1890 — perhaps at the Savile Club of which they were both members — and seems to have responded immediately to his down-to-earth rationalist beliefs and attitudes. During the succeeding years — those in which he published *Tess* and *Jude* and his first volumes of verse — Hardy often spent weekends at Clodd's house on the seafront at Aldeburgh, Suffolk, usually in company with a group of Clodd's other literary, scientific, and intellectual friends. To judge from Clodd's diaries, Hardy had the knack of making himself good company on these occasions; he took Clodd into his confidence perhaps to a greater extent than he did any other of his friends, and by the turn of the century it was recognized between them that Aldeburgh was for Hardy a convenient and pleasant refuge from the stresses of his marriage. Between 1909 and the sudden death of his first wife in November 1912 he sometimes took with him to Aldeburgh a young woman named Florence Dugdale, thirty-eight years his junior, who assisted him in various secretarial tasks and for whom he felt an increasingly strong emotional attachment. Florence Dugdale, meanwhile, confided a good deal in Clodd and wrote him a series of indiscreet letters about life at Max Gate, the Hardys' Dorset home, and especially about the quarrels between husband and wife she had witnessed while staying there.

These letters are in the Brotherton, as are several of Hardy's own letters to Clodd; a special interest of the letter illustrated is that is shows both Hardy's hand and Florence's, the latter having become the second Mrs Hardy on 10 February 1914. Hardy asks for Clodd's advice on investments, while Florence assures him that her first year of marriage has proved '*really & truly*' of '*great* happiness'.

The author and banker Edward Clodd (1840–1930) inspired the affection and confidence of numerous important people; the combination of his rigorously researched and argued rationalist views and his charming, generous personality were for many irresistible. Like Hardy, Meredith, Gissing, and Samuel Butler were good friends; scientific admirers included T. H. Huxley, Sir James G. Frazer, and Sir Edwin Ray Lankester. The Collection has many letters from all of them, manuscripts of Clodd's own work and heavily annotated copies of his publications.

Of our several other letter collections of this period, the largest is that of Clement Shorter, journalist, critic and collector of literary manuscripts. He also made many friends, but much of this correspondence is more business-like, from contributors to periodicals he edited, notably The Sphere. *There are smaller but substantial groups of letters to two earlier journal editors, G. A. Sala and Jabez Hogg. A collection of Bram Stoker's letters has some thousands of items, mostly directed to him not as the author of* Dracula *but as Sir Henry Irving's business manager at the Lyceum Theatre; so many include requests, evidently satisfied, for complimentary tickets that it is the more impressive that the theatre's takings under Stoker exceeded £2 million. There is another smaller collection relating to the drama, letters received by Henry Arthur Jones; with them is the manuscript of his play* Whitewashing Julia *(performed 1903).*

In my lay thought, if Europe is going scat, why not invest in America? But the brokers turn a cold shoulder to this idea apparently.

We have not heard a sound of you lately (though I read an article of yours in the D.C. a few days ago,) & hope you are both well. We are quite dormant at present, but ~~they~~ mean to wake up in the spring; when, or in early summer, we hope to see you here & Mrs Clodd.

Sincerely yours

Thomas Hardy.

To this I add affectionate greetings to you & your wife & hope that very soon, as soon as this dismal wintery weather is over, we may have the great pleasure of seeing you both at Max Gate. T. is like a dormouse & loves to be curled up in his study waiting for the spring. We have been married a year & a day, & really & truly (I

36. LENIN (1870–1924)

Autograph letter of introduction for Arthur Ransome, 7 February 1919.

Between 1917 and 1919 Arthur Ransome, special correspondent of the (London) *Daily News*, acquired a well-deserved reputation as the best-informed Western newspaperman in Russia: one of only two British journalists (the other being Morgan Philips Price, of the *Manchester Guardian*) with the *entrée* of the Bolshevik leadership. He had even fallen in love with Trotsky's secretary, Evgenia Shelepina, and subsequently married her. By the autumn of 1918 his activities had brought him into deep disfavour with the British government, then staging its tragi-comic intervention against Russia, but he remained determined to tell the truth about the Bolsheviks, as he saw it, to the British people. With this in mind he planned to write a history of the Revolution (never finished) and a report to the Foreign Office (which was ignored). He arrived in Moscow from Petrograd on 5 February 1919 and immediately applied to Lenin for permission to go everywhere and see everyone. Lenin and he had always got on well, so the outcome of his application was this letter, which requests that the bearer 'comrade Ransome' be given every assistance in obtaining the information he requires. Ransome made good use of it, as can still be discovered from his pamphlet *Six Weeks in Russia in 1919*, which he wrote on his return to England in the spring, and which sold in enormous numbers. It helped to rouse British opinion to demand an end to intervention.

Although best remembered for his children's books such as Swallows and Amazons, *published 1930, Arthur Ransome, who was born in Leeds, was for some years foreign correspondent in Russia for the* Daily News *and* Manchester Guardian. *A considerable archive remains; not only are there nearly 700 typescripts of cables he sent from 1916 to 1924 but also numerous documents associated with the Russian revolution including a signed typescript of Trotsky's* History of the October Revolution.

From miscellaneous essays and short articles, followed by studies in literary criticism, Ransome turned to creating English versions of traditional Russian folk tales, many of which survive in manuscript or typescript and have since been published. A keen sailor, in 1923 he wrote Racundra's First Cruise *based on his detailed logbooks; further logbooks exist for the other boats he owned before and after 'Racundra'. Two books on fishing, another favourite pursuit, appeared in 1929 and 1959. In between came the children's books, for which there are sets of Ransome's own original illustrations, and photographs of children acting out scenes from the books for Ransome to draw.*

Letters, diaries, photographs and newspaper cuttings constitute the remainder of the collection as it relates to Arthur Ransome. Further papers concerning Arthur's father, Cyril Ransome, are of interest partly on account of their Leeds connection, for he was Professor of Modern History and Literature from 1878 to 1896. Associated correspondence includes two particular subjects, Imperial Federation, and Prince Alamayu of Abyssinia, who died at Cyril Ransome's home in Leeds aged only eighteen.

The Ransome papers were presented to the Brotherton Collection in 1977 by Arthur Ransome's literary executors.

РОССІЙСКАЯ
ФЕДЕРАТИВНАЯ
СОВѢТСКАЯ РЕСПУБЛИКА.

ПРЕДСѢДАТЕЛЬ
СОВѢТА
НАРОДНЫХЪ КОМИССАРОВЪ.

Москва, Кремль.

7. II. 1919 г.

№

Народным

Комиссарам

и во все Советские

учреждения.

Рекомендую подателя,
товарища РЭНСОМА,
корреспондента английских
американских газет, и
прошу оказать ему всяче-
ское содействие для получения
интересующих его сведений.

Пр. СНК В. Ульянов (Ленин)

37. KEITH DOUGLAS (1920–44)

Autograph manuscript of an untitled autobiographical story, 1932.

Opening with the portentousness of a great biography, turning at once to irony and then to the charm and humour of childhood recollection, these sheets are the first two of thirteen torn from a notepad, the story on which is the only written record of Keith Douglas's earliest childhood. His mother remembered finding them in 1932, when he had returned to Christ's Hospital after a holiday. He was twelve. But as his earliest poems confirm, Douglas was astonishingly precocious. In this autobiographical story we find a vivid evocation of his first five years, and character sketches with a sharpness of observation which prefigures Douglas's classic narrative *Alamein to Zem Zem*, published in 1946. The characters in these pages are his immediate family: his rumbustious, soldierly father who is very much the hero of this, the only piece Douglas wrote about him; and his mother, whose late entry into the story transforms its whole mood and meaning. For while each event and character is authentic, Douglas moves his story through to a chilling conclusion, shaping and pacing it with that same 'fearlessness of imagination' which Geoffrey Hill was to find in his later work. *Later* work? Douglas was only twenty-four when he was killed in Normandy three days after the landings: but as a poet he had achieved a writing career of ten years. As a courageous and undeflected explorer of experience his career, as this story attests, was far longer.

The Keith Douglas section of the Collection is less rich in autograph manuscripts, of which nevertheless there are several, than in other material associated with the writer's brief life. We have many of the books he owned, often annotated by him, some rare printings of his work, drawings, numerous photographs and documents, and other memorabilia acquired from the Douglas family.

Most of the literary manuscripts in the Brotherton Collection of twentieth-century writers who made their reputations before the war in which Douglas died are by friends of Mrs McGrigor Phillips, who wrote herself under her first married name, Dorothy Una Ratcliffe. She was a generous friend to W. W. Gibson, of whose autograph poetry and correspondence we have a large collection, and likewise to Lascelles Abercrombie, a Leeds professor, represented here by many manuscripts of poetry and drama, and of literary criticism (added with financial assistance from the Arts Council of Great Britain). Mrs McGrigor Phillips acquired autograph poems from Sir William Watson, of whom she was a timely patron, and manuscripts of several verse plays and poems from another Yorkshire writer and friend, Gordon Bottomley. The manuscript of The Golden Apple *was purchased from Lady Gregory and a massive fair copy of* The Drunk Man Looks at the Thistle *from Hugh MacDiarmid, the only one in existence according to his note which accompanies it. Other large collections of work are by John Drinkwater (assembled by his secretary), the local poet Will Foster and Wilfred Rowland Childe, a Leeds University lecturer and Oxford acquaintance of Aldous Huxley. Naturally, the Collection has many manuscripts and much correspondence of Dorothy Una Ratcliffe herself.*

As a child he was a militarist, and like many of his warlike elders, built up heroic opinions upon little information, some scrappy ~~war~~ stories of his father. Most of the time he was down in the field, busy, with ~~the~~ an absurdly purposeful look on his round face, about a tent made of an old sheet, and sign-posted with a board saying 'sergeants' mess.' He was quite at home there for hours, while he was four and five, telling himself stories as he ran about, and sometimes stopping a moment to contemplate the calf who shared that field, a normally quiet animal, but given to jumping five-barred gates. As you would expect, he played with lead soldiers, & toy artillery, and was most fond of the cavalry and the highlanders. Unlike

the other troops who either marched sedately with sloped arms or sat bolt upright on their caracoling steeds, the highlanders were charging, their kilts flying at a swift angle out behind them and the plumes upon their heads also flying out, though often in the wrong direction for the broken heads were fixed back on with matches & swivelled easily.

His father did not spend very much time with him, but would speak to him of war and boxing & shew the boy his great muscles, for here at least he could shew them off to unbounded admiration. He teased his son, & pinched & tormented him sometimes, but Keir liked his ~~father~~ father better than his mother, who fondled him a deal too

38. JOHN COWPER POWYS (1872–1963)

Autograph letter to G. R. Wilson Knight, 12 October 1957.

The beginning and end of a letter by John Cowper Powys to G. Wilson Knight expressing his delight at Knight's article-review, under the title 'Cosmic correspondences', of Powys's *Up and Out* in the *Times Literary Supplement* of 11 October 1957. The full text of the slightly revised review and of the letter are published in *Powys to Knight*, edited by Robert Blackmore, 1983.

Knight had been corresponding with Powys since 1937 but the *Times Literary Supplement* in 1957 offered him the space to analyse the causes of his admiration. The review does not focus on *Up and Out*, but is rather an essay on the whole of Powys's work with a special concentration on *A Glastonbury Romance*, 1933, which had first aroused Knight's intense interest and which he acclaimed as 'the heart of Powys's work'. In that book, as the review states, 'we meet one of the strangest and most terrifying studies in fiction — the sadistic Mr Evans'. Powys responds in this letter 'Nobody but you has brought into an analysis of me as a writer the one essential thing — namely that I was born a sadist!'. But however sadistic his imaginings it should be noted that he confesses that as a boy 'the wickedest thing I ever did' was to chop up some earthworms. The philosophical support for the obsession of Mr Evans and his author is that the First Cause includes a malign as well as a benign aspect and function. It should also be noted that Powys became a fervent anti-vivisectionist.

Knight's penetrating analysis in 'Cosmic Correspondences' delighted J. C. Powys. Here was a reader 'a Prof who is also a psychiatrist and who is also a prophet . . . there's none like you'. Besides enriching a friendship, the long *TLS* review had much influence in establishing and extending the prestige which J. C. Powys's work now enjoys.

Professor G. R. Wilson Knight (1897–1985), the great Shakespeare critic, taught English Literature at Leeds University from 1946 until his extraordinarily active retirement began in 1962. The Brotherton Collection has many of his papers relating to all aspects and phases of his life, his work particularly on Shakespeare and on Byron, his own poetry and his virtuoso stage performances. Central to the collection is his vast correspondence with the poet Francis Berry (b. 1916), covering 50 years, of which we are fortunate to have both sides; these, like the many letters from Powys, are unusually revealing of their writer's work and ideas. We also have a great many manuscripts of Professor Berry's poetry and literary criticism, from pieces written in his mid-teens through to recent years.

Two other distinguished professors of the University have deposited in the Collection their letters from two twentieth-century critics of an eminence comparable to that of the late Professor Knight. Professor Bonamy Dobrée corresponded with T. S. Eliot throughout their long friendship; the resultant sequence of some 180 letters by Eliot from 1924 to 1963 is remarkable for its mingling of serious discussion and often playful informality. Professor William Walsh was a student of F. R. Leavis, later his friend and writer about him; we now have Dr Leavis's letters, and some from his wife Q. D. Leavis, written to Professor Walsh in the early 1970s.

1 Waterloo
Blaenau-Ffestiniog
Merionethshire
North Wales
Saturday Oct 12th 1957

yours devoted
old Boswell
& P. P. Jones
in respectful love.
J.C.P.

My dear Friend and Professor [I don't follow it]
Best of all possible Professors
It would take a third story to
up & out to do justice to
of the penetrating insight
of those searching eyes
of yours into my inmost soul. [INMOST]
Aye! but and I'm proud & vain &
I can only pray not to be the
conceited too! — amazing
subject of this
essay!

up & out

P.P. yours in respectful love

[I am puzzled why I deliberately inserted
that "and" after "but" following aye!
It must have been a reversion to some
very local dialectical habit in Derbyshire!
That's the only way I can explain it! but
I know I wanted to support, prob[ably] strengthen
build in, the "I'm proud"!

[O but I am so delighted with
this discourse of yours on me. It
couldn't be better.

39. ALAN ROSS (born 1922)

Typescript with autograph revisions of 'Palace of Culture, Sinaia', c. 1970.

The author writes:

I went on a lecture tour of Hungary and Roumania in the 60s and, accompanied by an ever-vigilant female shadow, was allowed to see some of the country. In Sinaia a formerly grand house belonging to a dissolute aristocrat had been turned into a writers' colony — where, as in the poem, selected writers were installed, required like battery-hens to produce. At weekends workers and trade union officials cavorted decorously among the pines.

The poem was first published, amidst others by Auden, Octavio Paz, Neruda, Enright, Plomer, and Porter, in the April/May 1971 issue of *London Magazine*, edited then as now by Alan Ross himself; relatively little of Mr Ross's own poetry has in fact appeared in his magazine. 'Palace of Culture, Sinaia' was then reprinted, the text unchanged, in Mr Ross's collection of poems *The Taj Express*, 1973. Manuscripts and typescripts of the other 50 poems in this volume are also in the Brotherton Collection, the variety of papers on which they are written — West Indian Post Office telegram forms, journalists' expense account forms, notepaper with various letter-heads — reflecting something of the vividly cosmopolitan nature of the poems themselves.

In his poem 'Library fire' (another manuscript in the Collection), Alan Ross writes of the books on his shelves 'They were like retainers, or old relatives / Slightly outstaying their welcome': his manuscripts in the Brotherton Collection find a new working life rather than honourable retirement.

Alan Ross's presence is constantly felt in the Brotherton Collection's archive of the papers from 1972 of the London Magazine, *which he has edited since 1961, succeeding John Lehmann. The archive, the largest single group of contemporary manuscripts in the Collection, consists of copy for the magazine; contributors' manuscripts or more frequently typescripts, often with various emendations; the printers' proofs of the magazine, with the authors' and sometimes the editor's corrections; and hundreds of letters from contributors concerning work submitted or on other matters, the personal friendship of the editor with many of them making this far more than a purely business correspondence over a dozen years.*

Reference to the printed volumes of the magazine will readily reveal the writers, artists and others who are represented in the archive, but one may mention large and interesting groups of material by Sir John Betjeman, Douglas Dunn, Gavin Ewart, Roy Fuller, Nadine Gordimer, Susan Hill, Philip Larkin, William Plomer, Anthony Powell, William Sansom, Stephen Spender, James Stern, and Julian Symons. There is much evidence also of Alan Ross's encouragement of younger writers like Graham Swift and William Boyd, his interest in the visual arts and his achievement in bringing to a British audience the work of writers from Eastern Europe, South America, India, Japan, Africa, and Australasia.

The Collection also has part of the publishing archive of Alan Ross's imprint London Magazine Editions, *including material relating to the publication of* The Loiners, *1970, by Tony Harrison, a Leeds University graduate.*

Access to the correspondence of living writers may be restricted at the discretion of the Keeper of the Brotherton Collection.

ALAN ROSS

PALACE OF CULTURE,

~~RUMANIA~~ SINAIA

In former days plump blondes,
Stepping from iced furs, tightened their buttocks
On the hands of drunk courtiers. Glass crashed.
Snow was a kind of madness
Mixed with blood and spilled vodka, harsh cries
Of officers on horseback. Swords glinted
In moonlight curdled on blue rivers,
Pines and birch upright as guardsmen.

A palace famed for debauchery,
Where sailors fresh from the Caspian
~~Thrust beards up the [illegible] of actresses~~ Roughed up the bodies of dancers
Now the rococo and mirrored ceilings,
Oceans of nudity, record the ~~careful~~ hairdos
Of secretaries, typing in triplicate -
Partings like fishbones, ~~grave~~ thighs
Woolly adhesive. In this museum,

Dedicated to detaching from the past
Its splendour, ~~the dead eyes of custodians~~
~~Roll like marbles.~~ Conformism has its deserts,
Ballrooms waltzing to railwaymen, the ~~lead clatter~~ woodpecker
Clatter Of compositors ~~tapping like woodpeckers~~, writers
Like battery-hens laying in captivity. ~~Here~~ In Sinaia
Effort is rewarded, contact with ~~an~~ corruption
~~An environment - eyes raised to onion domes~~
~~Of Sinaia like symbols of productivity -~~
A trophy for the enslaved, their tributes exacted.
Under these onion domes ~~of Sinaia~~, culture is obedience.

40. TOM PAULIN (born 1949)

Autograph manuscript draft of 'The Book of Juniper', 1979.

The author writes:

Mostly I can't remember when a poem got written, but for some reason I can call back various moments to do with the sequence that became 'The Book of Juniper'. I got invited to read poems at a conference in Vancouver in 1979 and I remember being annoyed by a representative from the Northern Irish Arts Council who kept insisting that the number of writers present from the North of Ireland clearly proved what a healthy culture it was that had nourished them. At the conference I met the Irish historian Roy Foster, who had written a book on Parnell and who shared my admiration for that distinguished revisionist, Conor Cruise O'Brien. When I got back to England I read Roy's book and various histories of Ireland, and lying in bed with flu sometime that winter, I began to day-dream about a small village on the coast of Donegal where I've spent holidays since about 1955. Off Naran Strand there's a treeless island called Iniskeel (Irish for Church Island) and when there's a spring tide you can walk out over the bared strand to the island. There's a graveyard, a derelict house, two holy wells and a ruined church — a very old building made of local ironstone. In the summer months I used to watch pilgrimages over the strand and wonder what penances the pilgrims performed, moving on bare knees between the holy wells and the cairns.

My poem began with thoughts of that island. I remember when Roy and his wife, Aisling, saw an early proof of it, they thought the closing lines somewhat nationalistic. Perhaps they are, I don't know. Anyway, the poem is much disliked in Belfast and the phrase about the sweet equal republic really annoys people. They point to Knock Airport, moving statues, Kerry babies. Maybe reality is on their side.

The Collection has several groups of manuscripts by Tom Paulin, who, though brought up in Northern Ireland, was born in Leeds. Three other contemporary poets from over the Irish Sea are represented here: Seamus Heaney by an autograph poem and an autobiographical piece, Paul Muldoon by a book of drafts for Mules, *1977, and 'Hugh Maxton', who taught here, by a variety of material.*

The authors of many modern manuscripts in the Collection share some connection with Leeds University. We have examples of work by all holders of the University's Gregory Fellowship in Poetry, many presented by the authors, with good representation of James Kirkup, Thomas Blackburn, Jon Silkin, Peter Redgrove and Paul Mills; an archive of the literary papers of Kevin Crossley-Holland, Fellow from 1969 to 1971, is very extensive. On leaving Leeds for Cambridge, Geoffrey Hill presented drafts of the text of the cantata Ad Incensum Lucernae, *later adapted in part for* Tenebrae, *1978. We also have work by former students, including Rayner Heppenstall (B.A. 1932) and Wole Soyinka (B.A. 1957); and literary papers of an honorary graduate, the late Norah Smallwood, are here, presented from her estate. But a Leeds connection is far from essential for inclusion in the Collection. Thus we have, for example, autograph drafts of Roy Fuller's memoirs, manuscripts of unpublished poems by George Barker and some writing by Craig Raine about himself.*

Juniper

In the original liturgy
on a bare island

a voice seeks an answer
in the sea wind:

'The tides parted and I crossed
barefoot to Brighthest.

Goose-grass and broken walls
were all my sanctuary.

On a thymey headland
I entered the strict soul

of a grasshopper—
heat haze and wild flowers,

a warm chirring all
that civil afternoon, on—

till its classic song
failed me and I sighed

for ~~another~~ — a different love
in grey weather.

*

Place the yeasty word
between my lips,

give me comfort
in a sheepfold,

shelter me
in a wild grove'.

*

'There is no word
and no comfort.

Only a blessed stone
is given you,

and juniper,
green juniper.'

*

Where was that gold cross,
the saint's treasure?

Or that spring of sweet water
—soft cleanness

grained silver-grey
branches

bare low
coward
cowardice

41. MARRICK PRIORY

Manuscript map of Marrick, North Yorkshire, 1592.

The 'platt' reproduced is one of a number of maps portraying the possessions of the former Priory at Marrick in 1592 when the estate was sold. A very distorted sketch-map, it nevertheless illustrates many features of the estate, including the Priory site (*marrig abbaie*), shown as a cluster of buildings by means of ten triangles, and also the limits of the land first granted, with the pre-existing church, to the nuns. These limits extended from *almepole* in the River Swale northwards by *threllesgate*, then eastwards along the side of *heleinsleie bargh alias weinesbarghe* to where the tofts (houses) of the church adjoined the tofts of Marrick and thence by the heads of the crofts of the vill (*towne croftes*) to the beck (*rounelette sike*) running into the road from *baccestane grave*, and by the beck to the Swale.

This initial grant, like later ones of lands lying intermingled in the open-fields with those of Marrick Manor, carried rights in common pastures. Beneath these common pastures were veins of mineral ores which in places approached the surface. Such was the vein or *gang* known as *Copperthwaite* which had long been exploited for its lead; hence the swathe of pit-shafts at *Copperthwaite gang* and, to the south on the wind-swept fell side, the five *bales*, 'hills' or mounds of stone, fuel and ore for smelting lead, among them the *priores bale* (Priory's bail).

Marrick in 1592 was a substantial village with dwellings, represented by triangles, on all four sides of *Marrig towne grene*. The church, however, remained at *marrig abbaie*, three-quarters of a mile distant and so far below the village that the direct way going steeply down past the *smithie*, and through now enclosed fields, led into a long flight of stone-slab steps.

Lord Brotherton saw his personal library as a national rather than local collection, but it was natural that he should wish to acquire some material with a strong Yorkshire connection. While the University has been responsible for developing the Collection, a Yorkshire element has remained, on occasions, a very welcome feature of an item, if seldom its main reason for acquisition.

The largest group of Yorkshire manuscripts relates to the estates of Marrick Priory, a Benedictine foundation in Swaledale, which was for centuries an important lead-mining area. There are documents from the twelfth century onwards, the majority concerning ownership of the lands from the surrender of the Priory's possessions to Henry VIII in 1539 through to the nineteenth century. A number of items have good impressions of royal seals attached. Many of the other Yorkshire deeds present are of the seventeenth and eighteenth centuries, relating to local possessions of the second Duke of Buckingham, Strafford, Sir Robert Clayton and the Fairfaxes. There are also a few items of Fairfax family correspondence and a manuscript compilation of family history, 'Analecta Fairfaxiana', c. *1660. Miscellaneous material includes the antiquarian papers of Lord Brotherton's acquaintance Carus Vale Collier (1864–1929), a document signed by Guy Fawkes concerning the disposition of his property, and a rent book of the Fauconberg estate recording Laurence Sterne's annual payment of £6 for Shandy Hall, 1760–68.*

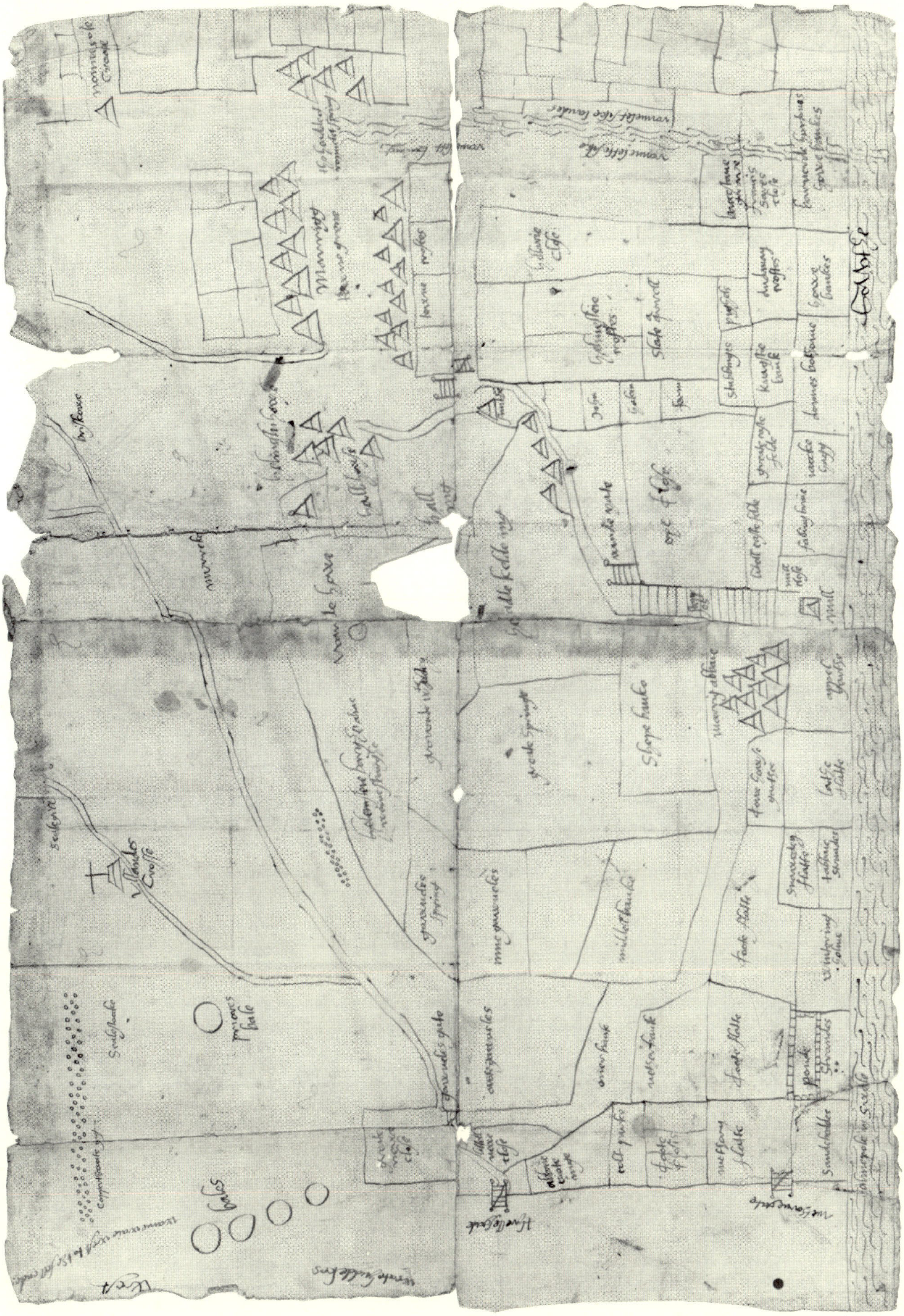

42. RALPH THORESBY (1658–1725)

Autograph letter to Joseph Smith, 22 April 1723.

Ralph Thoresby was the son of a pious Leeds cloth merchant with strong antiquarian interests. Brought up to follow in his father's footsteps, and sent to commercial houses in London and abroad to learn his father's trade, Ralph Thoresby nevertheless did not take kindly to business or prosper in it. Instead he followed intellectual pursuits, building up a large museum collection and maintaining an extensive correspondence on antiquarian matters with many of the most learned luminaries of his day; in recognition of his scholarly eminence he became a Fellow of the Royal Society in 1697. By the age of 40 he had withdrawn from merchanting to concentrate on the study of antiquities, notably local history. His *Ducatus Leodiensis* was published in 1715. A topography of Leeds with transcripts and long historical and genealogical digressions, this volume was the first historical work of any kind to be published on Leeds, and it recorded much material unavailable elsewhere.

Following the practice of the day Thoresby had himself supervised the printing and publication of his book, working on the proofs at the printer's and fretting about the slow progress. By 1720 he was putting the finishing touches to another part of his project, a history of the church in Leeds, based on manuscript records of the clergy. In 1723 he negotiated terms with his London printer, Joseph Smith of Exeter-Change (near the Fountain Tavern in the Strand) and undertook once more the wearying business of seeing the manuscript through the press, a task made more troublesome by his failing health. In his diary for the ensuing month he again complained repeatedly of delays and neglect by the printer and his workmen, giving vent to his impatience in letters, such as the example shown, to Smith himself. By December, however, advance copies were ready, and Thoresby's *Vicaria Leodiensis* was published in 1724; Smith's bill totalled £11 5s. 10d. for fifty-four copies in differing bindings.

Thoresby may be the greatest of Leeds's local historians, but the number of those who have written on Yorkshire is vast and our Collection has hundreds of their printed works. One of our copies of Thoresby's Ducatus *is annotated with early notes on the fate, often consignment to the dunghill, of the contents of his museum. Barnsley, Doncaster, and Rotherham, besides Leeds, are well covered in the Collection and we have examples of Yorkshire printing and local dialect poetry. But the greatest emphasis is on Sheffield material, for Lord Brotherton acquired much of the library of W. T. Freemantle, compiler of* A Bibliography of Sheffield . . . to the end of 1700, *1911. As well as most of the Freemantle books noted in the published bibliography, we have also his much larger collections and his notes for its projected continuations into the twentieth century, which were never published. The range of Sheffield pamphlets is especially wide and the city's poets James Montgomery and Ebenezer Elliott are very well represented; the many editions of Montgomery's works include several copies of his* The Whisperer, *1798, of which he tried to destroy every example, and there are presentation copies of Elliott's works, together with some autograph letters and manuscripts by him.*

Mr Smith

I am sory to have renewed occasions of complaint, but no man living can endure such treatment I have waited at the Printers an hower this morning & not only Mr Hunter is in the Country, but Mr Hills the compositor cannot be found, all the rest are at their works, & my book alone is at a full stand. none to proceed in it, I have left a reprimand but all I beleive to no purpose. If you do not remedy it speedily I must take another method, not so agreeable to Sr

22 April munday morning past 9

Your humble servt but
forgotten friend
Ralph Thoresby

43. EDMUND WALLER (1606–87)

Autograph letter to Henry Marten, 1643.

Of Edmund Waller, greatly admired as a poet by his contemporaries, Douglas Bush wrote in 1945 'No poetical reputation of the seventeenth century has been so completely and irreparably eclipsed'. However, in personal rather than literary life, Waller had, in the eyes of many, no good reputation to lose. The reason for this lay in his conduct after the discovery in 1643 of 'Waller's plot'.

A Member of Parliament since his teens, Waller had for long resisted taking sides in the deepening dispute between Charles I and Parliament, when in early 1643 he became involved in an abortive plot on the King's behalf. Royalists in London were to be mobilised in concert with an outside attack to seize the city for the King. However, in May the plot was betrayed, Waller was arrested and thereupon he promptly accused and informed on his fellow conspirators in the hope of saving his own life. Others were hanged, but Waller himself, far wealthier than is common with poets, paid a £10,000 fine and, after expulsion from Parliament and a year in the Tower, went into exile in Paris. In 1651 he was pardoned, but to many his self-preservation remained unforgiveably contemptible.

In this letter we see something of the desperation of Waller's attempts to avoid punishment for his plotting, for it is addressed to Henry Marten, one of the King's most uncompromising parliamentary opponents. Indeed, that Waller should even consider appealing to Marten is a measure of the latter's reputation for generosity; as John Aubrey wrote of Marten, 'He was . . . a great cultor of justice and did always in the House take the part of the oppressed.'. Ironically, Marten himself was expelled from Parliament a month after Waller, and was briefly in the Tower, not for plotting for Charles but for being too outspoken against him.

Waller's letter is from a substantial collection of political, legal, and estate papers of the regicide Henry Marten (1602–80), his father, the prominent lawyer Sir Henry Marten (1562?–1641) and the Loder-Symonds family. The Martens' manor of Hinton Waldrist, used as security for a loan by Henry Marten, was acquired by John Loder in the late 1660s. Some of this material, the largest group of historical documents in the Brotherton Collection (other than Yorkshire deeds), is described in Historical Manuscripts Commission, 13th Report, appendix, part IV, *1892, pp. 378–404; several listed items, however, are not now present.*

Other British political papers include some 200 letters, mostly from the 1780s, written to Thomas Townshend, first Viscount Sidney (1733–1800) and, in smaller number, to his father and to his eldest son; letters, formerly in the Morrison Collection, written by the 2nd, 3rd, and 5th Dukes of Leeds; and letters and other manuscripts sent to the 1st and 2nd Viscounts Melville, including the latter's correspondence with the Earl of Minto, 1807–12.

Our large collection of the papers of the Chevalier D'Éon (1728–1810), spy, diplomat and transvestite, includes correspondence with John Wilkes, Beaumarchais and others, and much of D'Éon's compulsive autobiographical writing. Another extensive historical source, printed rather than manuscript, comprises over 550 contemporary pamphlets and tracts concerning the unsuccessful Brabant revolution of 1789–90.

Noble Sr

you have vouchsafed to looke
upon me in my distress & as you
have descended to a worke of mercy
so I knowe you will take care
that I shall not now (after a seeming
favour in having ben so longe
reserved) have the disadvantage
to be tryed by bare examinations &
confessions wthout the power of
cross examination of wittnesses,
there being none but such as are
condemned already: my humble &
as I thinke my iust request is
a tryall att Comon lawe or att
least a hearing by my Councill why
I should so be tryed (Sr) remember
what I have ben & by Gods favour
moving your hearts, may yet be.
lett not the blood of so faithfull
a frend be vile in yr eyes

I hope God (who knowes what I would have done
to redeeme yr life from danger) will move
you to give some desire to yr most humble & most faithfull
servant [illegible]

44. VISCOUNT SNOWDEN (1864–1937)

Autograph text of the Budget radio broadcast, 28 April 1931.

Philip Snowden was born at Ickornshaw in West Yorkshire, the son of a weaver. His birthplace, he wrote, 'was on the edge of the Brontë country. A few miles of wild moorland separated my parish from Haworth'. Crippled following a cycling accident, he was invalided out of the Civil Service in 1893. He began to study socialism during his convalescence and for a decade after 1895 settled down to a career as a propagandist for the Independent Labour Party. First becoming a Member of Parliament in 1906, he sat for nearly a quarter of a century as a Labour Member. He was appointed Chancellor of the Exchequer in Ramsay MacDonald's cabinet of 1924, and again in MacDonald's second cabinet of 1929. This was the third occasion on which a Chancellor of the Exchequer made a broadcast statement on the Budget.

Snowden was an Independent Labour Party candidate in the Wakefield by-election of 1902 which was won by Lord (then Mr Edward A.) Brotherton. Snowden described his opponent in *An Autobiography* (1934) as 'a charming man personally — gentle, kind and generous. He knew nothing whatever about politics, and his platform appearances were described by a local newspaper, strongly opposing my candidature, as a gross exhibition of political ignorance. That they may have been, but they were certainly the most entertaining speeches I have ever had to deal with in a political contest'. Snowden received the honorary degree of Doctor of Laws from the University of Leeds in 1927, and his bust by Ströbl is in the Brotherton Library. He was created Viscount on 24 November 1931. This manuscript was presented to the Brotherton Collection by his widow and finds a natural place in the collection of books and manuscripts gathered together by Alf Mattison.

Alf Mattison (1868–1944) was born and lived in Leeds, where he worked in an engineering-shop and later moved to a clerical post in the Leeds City Transport Department. At 17 he joined William Morris's Socialist League, was later befriended by Edward Carpenter and in 1893 attended the inaugural conference of the Independent Labour Party at Bradford. A life-long socialist, Mattison became a trusted friend of important labour leaders and activists. Probably his own major achievement was collecting many published and unpublished writings illustrative of the progress of British socialism and, though a political opponent, Lord Brotherton had the vision to acquire the collection for his library.

The manuscript section of Mattison's collection includes some 50 family letters of the Owenite radical J. F. Bray (1809–99), whose formative years were spent in Leeds, papers of John Lister, first treasurer of the I.L.P., and manuscript minutes of the 1893 Bradford conference. Mattison's personal papers include his diary-notebooks and over 300 letters from Carpenter, with several other Carpenter manuscripts. There are about 1,000 printed books varying in rarity, some being annotated and presentation copies, and a large collection of ephemeral pamphlets, periodicals and reports, some now very scarce, concerned with many labour causes; a special subject index to these printed works has been prepared. Mattison also carefully assembled newspaper cuttings on numerous people and on topics such as the General Strike.

2

of the Budget from "A well informed correspondent" whose information is based upon or nothing more substantial than a fertile imagination

Now you know the worst — No doubt most of you are greatly relieved, and even if you are affected by the small addition to your taxation, you can console yourself by the reflection that it might have been much worse. = Your income tax still remains at the old "modest" figure, your tobacco & beer will cost you no more, ~~and~~ I have, for this year at least, turned a deaf ear [ ] though much obliged for the suggestions & for the desire to help me ~~with~~ ~~[illegible]~~ in my

the teetolers and non-smokers still enjoy the reward of their virtues

Treasury Chambers,
Whitehall, S.W.

45. GEORGE BORROW (1803–81)

Autograph letter to Dawson Turner, 15 February 1842.

This letter is the earliest extant from George Borrow to Dawson Turner (1775–1858), an affluent botanist and antiquary who was resident at Great Yarmouth for most of his life. It is still accompanied by the autograph letter from the Gypsy of Cordova, Antonio Salazar, to which it refers and of which Borrow had inserted a translation in *The Zincali*.

During the years of his friendship with Turner, Borrow enjoyed much kind hospitality at the beautiful house on the South Quay at Yarmouth. As he wrote to his publisher, John Murray, after a visit there 'What capital port he keeps. He gave me some twenty years old and of nearly the finest flavour I ever tasted. There are few better things than old books, old pictures and old port and he seems to have plenty of all three'. By the time Borrow came to know him, a passion for manuscripts and autograph letters had long been superimposed on Turner's early interests in botanical studies and Norfolk antiquities. He said he would prize the gift of the Gypsy's letter among the principal treasures of his collection, and Borrow followed it with other similar donations, including a large section of *The Bible in Spain*. Turner tried to persuade Borrow to inject some order into his manuscripts, against the day when other eyes would examine them. In the end, however, those Borrow papers have been scattered all over the world, and the Brotherton Collection is but one of the fifty different repositories which now house them.

The Romany Collection, one of the largest devoted to the subject in this country, was originally formed by Lord Brotherton's niece-in-law Mrs D. U. McGrigor Phillips, who was intensely interested in the history and life of Gypsies. She presented the Romany Collection to the University in 1950 and continued to support it until her death in 1967, providing an endowment which still develops it. A Catalogue of the Romany Collection *was published in 1962, with over 1,200 entries arranged in broad subject groups, and there have been many additions since then.*

Besides the letter illustrated there are several Borrow manuscripts in the Collection, including notes and drafts of parts of The Bible in Spain, Lavengro, Romano Lavo-Lil *and* The Romany Rye, *as well as linguistic notes and folk tales. However, the largest group of manuscripts is a series of over 30 notebooks compiled by T. W. Thompson, for many years a major figure in the Gypsy Lore Society; they record meetings with travellers, recount many of their tales and legends and give extensive genealogical details. Further manuscripts and letters are present in the hands of other leading British Romany scholars, including F. H. Groome, Scott Macfie, John Sampson, Walter Starkie and especially Dora Yates, Mrs McGrigor Phillips's great ally in forming her Collection and later its Honorary Consultant. Manuscript poems on Gypsy topics include one by Arthur Symons and, by contrast, more recent additions include a section of the archives of the National Gypsy Council, presented by Dr Donald Kenrick.*

161.

Oulton · Lowestoft
Feb. 15 1842

My Dear Sir.

I send you according to promise the letter of the Cordovese Gypsy; you will find a translation of it in the first volume of my "Gypsies of Spain" p 253 I have always considered it as a highly curious and characteristic composition, on which account I feel most happy in presenting it to you, knowing as I do the great interest which you take in these things; I avail myself of the present opportunity to return you my most sincere thanks for the kindness and hospitality which I experienced at your hands when last at Yarmouth, and with kind remembrances to Mrs Turner

I have the honor to remain
My Dear Sir
Ever Most Truly Yours
George Borrow

Dawson Turner Esqr.

46. ALEXANDER PUSHKIN (1799–1837)

Tsygany (The Gypsies), *Moscow, 1827.*

Alexander Pushkin's *Tsygany (The Gypsies)*, composed between January and October 1824, was the last of his early narrative poems written under the influence of Byron's work during a lengthy political exile in Russia's southern provinces. The Gypsy theme was unusual in Russian literature at that time, but Pushkin was suitably prepared to broach it, having spent a month in a Bessarabian Gypsy encampment during the summer of 1821. The exotic local colour he was consequently able to apply in the poem appealed to the Romantic tastes of his readers, as did the somewhat melodramatic plot, loosely based on a true incident. The wanderer Aleko, disillusioned with civilisation, is given refuge by Gypsies, and is captivated by the enchanting Zemfira. Yet he can neither accept the easy morality of the Gypsies, nor allow others the liberty he craves for himself, is finally driven to murder the unfaithful Zemfira and her lover, and again becomes an outcast. The idealised lifestyle of the Gypsies is symbolic of the poem's central concern, the quest for personal freedom, a theme which ensured its success among the organisers of the ill-fated 'Decembrist' revolt against the autocracy of 1825. Their circulation of the work in manuscript delayed its publication until 1827, though several extracts appeared beforehand in periodicals, including the adaptation of a Moldavian Gypsy song which Pushkin incorporated in the text. Both this song individually and subsequently the poem as a whole were translated into English by Pushkin's acquaintance George Borrow.

In her foreword to the published catalogue of our Romany Collection, Dora Yates remarked on the variety of topics to which researchers would find reference in it — 'philology, ethnology and anthropology, history, music or art'. So wide is the range of printed books present, unified by their Romany aspects, that it is easy to add to this list: religion, sociology, education, and more.

We have works in some 30 languages or dialects, including at least a dozen forms of Romany. Indeed, the language of Gypsies has itself been a topic studied for centuries, from Die Rotwelsch Grammatic *(our edition is* c. *1520), through the later canting dictionaries including that of E.B., 1699, to the great works of twentieth-century scholarship. Their language has been but one of the distinctive features making Gypsies the object of suspicion and persecution from non-travelling populations. We have many historical records of their legal and other regulation, from early statutes and edicts of several countries (including one of Henry VIII) to accounts of their fate under the Nazis. The self-confessed rogue Bampfylde-Moore Carew, whose works are here in eleven early editions together with notes and correspondence of his modern editor C. H. Wilkinson, was not actually a Gypsy and the facts of the notorious Elizabeth Canning case, disputed in several contemporary pamphlets including Fielding's, remain unclear.*

A more positive view of Romany life, history and culture is expressed in numerous classic works in the Collection by Groome, Leland, Macfie, Miss Yates, and others, and we have first editions of most of Borrow's works. We constantly add to them and to our collection of press cuttings dating back to the seventeenth century.

ЦЫГАНЫ.

(Писано въ 1824 году).

МОСКВА.

ВЪ ТИПОГРАФІИ АВГУСТА СЕМЕНА,
при Императорской Мед.-Хирур. Академіи.

1827.

47. FELIX MENDELSSOHN-BARTHOLDY (1809–47)

Autograph manuscript of his sonata for piano in B flat minor, 1823.

The manuscript has 211 bars of music on three pages, the last verso of the bifolium blank. It is unsigned but the hand corresponds to Mendelssohn's signed works of the period, without yet the distinctive clefs of his mature hand. Note the archaic disposition of the key-signatures. Mendelssohn's characteristic motto 'L.e.g.G' ['Lass es gelingen, Gott'] appears at the top right of the first page, illustrated. The heading was originally 'Sonatina' and the date 27 November 1823 appears at the end. There are several corrections, and the second page lacks nearly all dynamics; the composer must have abandoned the work before polishing it or adding the further movements normal to a sonata.

The movement is in a standard sonata form, with slow introduction and repeated exposition. The fourteen-year-old composer was in full command of the serious post-classical sonata style and handles it with some passion and marked concentration; these appear respectively in the sighing motive of the Adagio, and in the motivic concentration of the Allegro (itself audibly linked to the Adagio). That the music is not childish is also indicated by the wide stretch of both hands (Allegro, right hand, 6th bar; left hand, 7 bars from the end of p. 1). Just under two years elapsed before the fully mature octet in E flat for Strings Op. 20.

The autograph is the only source for this sonata, which is missing from published catalogues of Mendelssohn's music. An edition prepared by R. Larry Todd was published in 1981 (C. F. Peters Corporation, New York: Edition Peters 66853).

Much of the musical material in the Collection comes from the library which Lord Brotherton acquired from W. T. Freemantle of Rotherham. Freemantle's extensive collection of material on Mendelssohn was the labour of many years. Besides the item illustrated, there are in all some 15 autograph manuscripts, with several more pieces for piano including a fair copy of the 'Gondellied'. We also have some 70 of Mendelssohn's autograph letters, mostly to Ignaz Moscheles, transcriptions of further Mendelssohn manuscripts, often made by Freemantle from borrowed originals, and numerous printed items, including a full score of St Paul *evidently annotated in Mendelssohn's hand for performance.*

Freemantle's other great musical interest was Charles Dibdin (1745–1814), the prolific song-writer and dramatist; thus we have a large accumulation of Dibdin's autograph manuscripts and many printed works, including dozens of songs. Other important eighteenth-century items include a copy of Arianna a Naxos, *jointly published by Haydn with John Bland, London 1791, signed by the composer with a fragment of autograph music pasted in; a manuscript anthem by William Croft; and early printed works by Arne, Corelli, and Handel. Rather earlier is Thomas Mace's* Musicks Monument, *1676, and later a great quantity of miscellaneous nineteenth-century printed music and a few manuscripts; in this later period Freemantle had special interest in Berlioz and, because of the Sheffield connection, in Sterndale Bennett.*

Musical material from other, non-Freemantle sources includes, besides the Novello papers, recent manuscripts of Peter Racine Fricker, Kenneth Leighton, and Richard Rodney Bennett, presented by the composers, and a sixteenth-century manuscript ballad.

Sonatina
Adagio
mf
p
f
p
dim.
Allegro non troppo.
dolce
p
f
p
f
p
f
p
mf
p
p
f
dim.
p
a piacere
1mo
1mo

48. JOHN GOULD (1804–81)

The birds of Great Britain. *5 volumes, London, 1873 [1862–73].*

John Gould's career illustrates admirably Victorian virtues and the ethics of business success. The son of a gardener, with little formal education, he started life as a trainee gardener at Windsor Castle, where he picked dandelions for the Queen's herbal tea; moved to the gardens at Ripley Castle in Yorkshire; but then in his early twenties secured the post of taxidermist to the Zoological Society of London. He became a successful ornithologist, gaining an F.R.S. for his discoveries in Australia, but made his name and his financial success by publishing the lavishly illustrated bird books of which the Brotherton Collection is fortunate to possess a fine selection. Gould's method was to make a rough sketch of the adult bird, preferably with young, in a natural pose; to commission the finished painting from an expert illustrator such as Edward Lear or Joseph Wolf; and to have the painting transferred to the lithographic stone by another specialist.

The illustration opposite is one of the finest examples of this teamwork from Gould's *The birds of Great Britain.* The painter was Wolf, who came from the Moselle valley in West Germany but settled in London as a free-lance artist; the lithographer was Henry Constantine Richter. The birds are the typical white morphs of the gyrfalcon (*Falco rusticolus candicans*), normally resident in arctic Greenland but occasionally finding their way to Britain. In Gould's day this morph was believed to be a separate species and given its own name. The adult bird is pictured on the right, and the young bird in the centre. Wolf shared Lear's passion for the details of plumage, and Audubon's virtuosity in presenting white birds against striking backgrounds.

In all we have five of Gould's bird books in 20 volumes, the bequest of Mr Charles Ratcliffe Brotherton (1882–1949). Amongst other superbly illustrated natural historical works, we have Edwards's Natural History of Uncommon Birds, *1743–51, Thornton's* Temple of Flora, *an edition of 1812, and Redouté's* Les Roses, *1817–24; Humphry Repton's* Observations on . . . Landscape Gardening, *1803, is in the original pink boards. Indeed, as with fine printing, there are finely illustrated books and manuscripts and other items related to the visual arts throughout the Collection.*

Numerous massive extra-illustrated works have abundant added engravings, drawings and watercolours plundered from many sources; expanded topographical works by Thomas Pennant, for example, are particularly replete and accounts by Bates and Thackeray of George Cruikshank include original work by him and many unusual engravings. More conventional are a proof set of illustrations for the Book of Job by Blake and other works illustrated by him.

The Romany section of the Collection has two oil paintings of Gypsy encampments from the 1790s by George Morland and some watercolours by Fred Lawson. Some earlier watercolour landscapes are said to be by John Varley and we have Richard Westall's original coloured designs for the engravings which appeared in an 1819 edition of The Arabian Nights. *Manuscript material includes long series of letters by the sculptor Sir Francis Chantrey and by Sir David Wilkie, the latter with one of his sketch books; and the autograph manuscript of Walter Crane's* An Artist's Reminiscences, *1904.*

49. WALTER CRANE (1845–1915)

Original design for an illustration in William Morris's The Story of the Glittering Plain. *1894.*

In the complete set of Kelmscott Press books in the Brotherton Collection, the most important association volume is the second edition of William Morris's *The Story of the Glittering Plain*, 1894, with illustrations by Walter Crane. Morris reprinted the volume after receiving twenty-three illustrations that were completed too late for the 1891 edition. It is the only Kelmscott title to have been printed twice. The Brotherton copy is boxed and its particular interest is that included within the box are three of Walter Crane's original designs, done in pen and brush with black ink and touches of white tempera, for the illustrations that were cut on wood for the edition by Crane's cousin, A. Leverett. The book itself has Crane's own signature on the inside of its front cover.

In his autobiography *An Artist's Reminiscences*, 1907, Crane recalls 'Morris and his friend, Mr. F. S. Ellis, who edited several of the Kelmscott Press books, coming to my studio to see the drawings for the *Glittering Plain* when they were finished'. According to his secretary Sydney Cockerell, Morris was 'dissatisfied . . . with Crane's illustrations . . . & thought this volume his one Kelmscott Press failure', though Morris himself wrote to Crane in February 1894 saying that his 'woodcuts look delightful'.

If Morris thought The Story of the Glittering Plain *his press's one failure, the Kelmscott Chaucer was seen as its triumph; the Collection has two copies of the latter in a set of the publications of the Kelmscott Press which also includes the specimen pages of Froissart's* Chronicles, *1897, printed on vellum. (We also have, incidentally, two incunabula owned by Morris himself and a very large unpublished manuscript* The Story of Olaf the Holy, *translated from the Icelandic by Eiríkr Magnússon and then entirely reworked by Morris.) Other modern private presses well represented are the Ashendene, Chiswick, Doves, Scholartis, and Vale, though we have examples of the work of many more.*

The pamphlets devised by T. J. Wise form one of the less noble enterprises of private printing history; the Collection has a number of examples and much correspondence of Wise referring to bibliographical matters.

Arguably, there is British and European fine printing almost everywhere in the Collection, but here we may particularly mention Baskerville and Foulis books and the great edition of Hume's History of England, *1806, printed by Bensley for Richard Bowyer using Joseph Jackson's types. We have lavishly extra-illustrated copies of several works by Thomas Frognall Dibdin, with his own working-copy of the first volume of his revision of Ames's* Typographical Antiquities, *1810, packed with his correspondence about it and including an original leaf of printing by Caxton. A similarly much-extended set of Timperley's* Encyclopaedia of Literary and Typographical Anecdote, *1842, is another such treasure-trove for all periods, especially rich in nineteenth-century printed ephemera.*

50. A TRAVELLING LIBRARY

A box resembling a single folio book, containing 43 small volumes, 1617.

This Jacobean travelling library is one of four of a similar kind, the others being in the British Library, the Huntington Library and the Toledo Museum of Art, Ohio. When closed, it appears to be a single leather-bound volume measuring 16 inches by 11, but once opened it is revealed to be a wooden box with three shelves containing 43 small books, vellum-bound and mostly printed in Leyden. A catalogue of the books faces them on the inside of the cover, painted in three columns surrounded by an arch design bearing a crest and five coats of arms. Each column relates to a shelf, one for Theology and Philosophy, one for History, one for Poetry.

The largest of the coats of arms is of an unidentified member of the Madden family, evidently the person to whom the travelling library first belonged. It was for long supposed that all four examples were made for Sir Julius Caesar (1558–1636), Master of the Rolls, to present to friends, because his Roman namesake's name is given special emphasis in the catalogue and Sir Julius did own the British Library example. However, H. M. Nixon and W. A. Jackson, to whose work all students of these travelling libraries are indebted, argued convincingly that they were all in fact commissioned by William Hakewill (1574–1655), traces of his name and arms dated January 1617 being just visible at the back of the bottom shelf of the Brotherton Collection's box. Who made the boxes and bound their contents is unknown, but there is evidence of a common source and a connection with the King's Printer, John Bill.

Lord Brotherton rarely acquired books or manuscripts primarily for their bindings, but the travelling library is an exception to the rule. So too is the remarkable collection of bindings originally executed at the turn of this century for Lord Howard de Walden by Rivière and Son, a series of over 100 beautifully crafted facsimiles and freer imitations of early bindings made for genuine early books. Sometimes the Howard de Walden books themselves were too eagerly renovated by the binder and some bindings are disconcertingly inappropriate, but together they form a magnificent survey of binding styles, unusually fresh and vivid for eyes more used to bindings mellowed by age.

We also have some authentic bindings by notable English binders. The attribution of one binding to Mary Collet of Little Gidding must be viewed more sceptically than that of a couple to the Mearne bindery. A trio of Settle presentation bindings includes one which still awaits his addition of a coat of arms. Later there are bindings by Roger Payne, Kalthoeber, and Edwards of Halifax. The outstanding twentieth-century example is probably a Kelmscott Chaucer bound, to a design by Morris himself, by Cobden-Sanderson, but there is further work by him and, for example, by Katherine Adams and by the Cockerell bindery. There are also many early European bindings, particularly of incunabula, which would repay closer study than has yet been undertaken; three fifteenth-century German chained bindings are on medieval manuscripts.

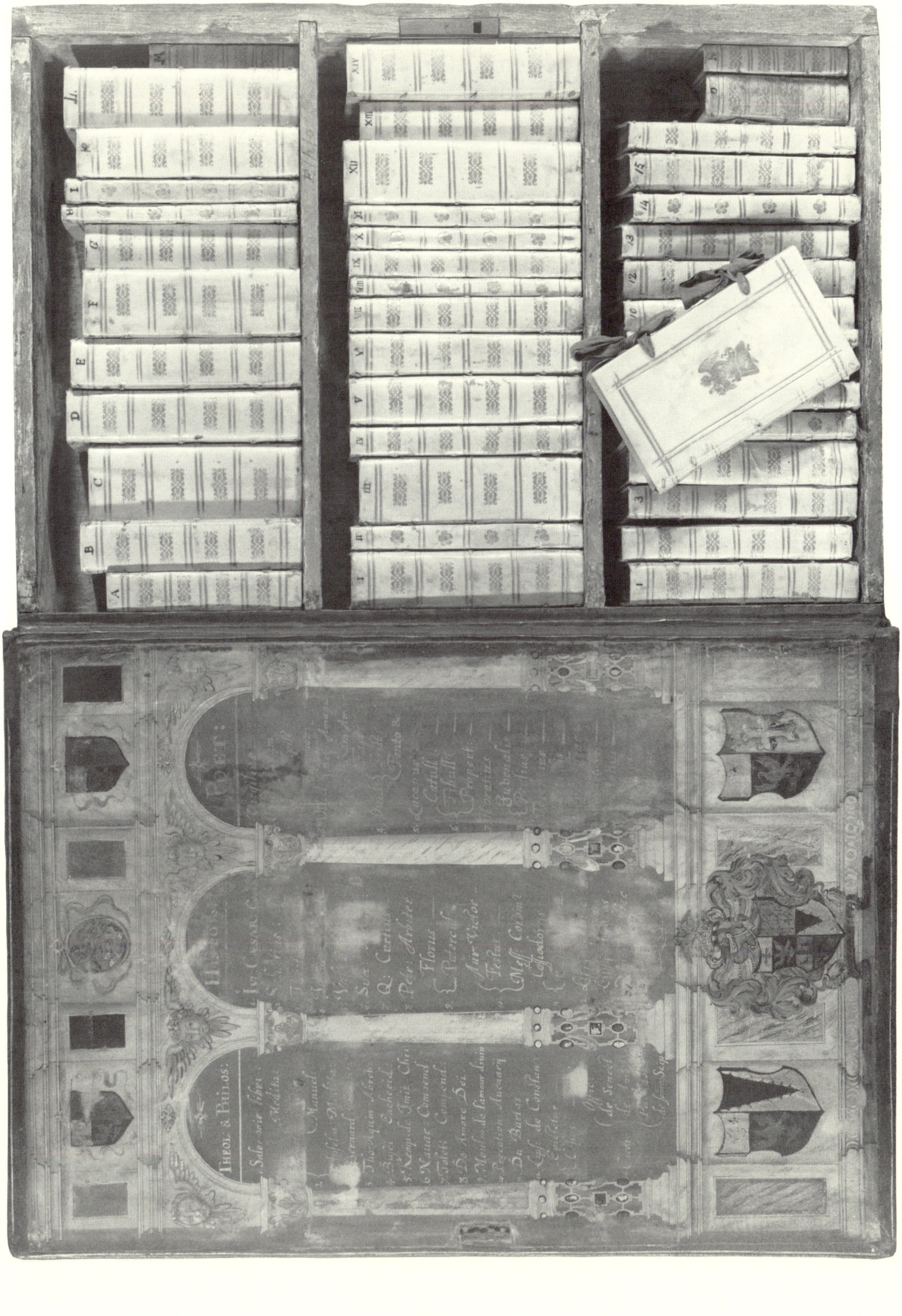

Index